Treatment
Strategies
for Abused
Children

Interpersonal Violence: The Practice Series

Jon R. Conte, Series Editor

Interpersonal Violence: The Practice Series is devoted to mental health, social service, and allied professionals who confront daily the problem of interpersonal violence. It is hoped that the knowledge, professional experience, and high standards of practice offered by the authors of these volumes may lead to the end of interpersonal violence.

In this series...

Treatment Strategies for Abused Children
From Victim to Survivor

Cheryl L. Karp
Traci L. Butler

Foreword by William N. Friedrich

Interpersonal Violence:
The Practice Series

SAGE Publications
International Educational and Professional Publisher
Thousand Oaks   London   New Delhi

For information address:

SAGE Publications, Inc.
2455 Teller Road
Thousand Oaks, California 91320
E-mail: order@sagepub.com

SAGE Publications Ltd.
6 Bonhill Street
London EC2A 4PU
United Kingdom

SAGE Publications India Pvt. Ltd.
M-32 Market
Greater Kailash I
New Delhi 110 048 India

Printed in the United States of America

Library of Congress Cataloging-in-Publication Data

Karp, Cheryl L.
    Treatment strategies for abused children: from victim to
survivor / authors, Cheryl L. Karp, Traci L. Butler.
        p.   cm.—(Interpersonal violence: the practice series; v. 13)
    Includes bibliographical references and index.
    ISBN 0-8039-7217-2 (acid-free paper).—ISBN 0-8039-7218-0
(pbk.: acid-free paper).
        1. Abused children—Rehabilitation. 2. Sexually abused children—
Rehabilitation. 3. Child psychotherapy. I. Butler, Traci L. II. Title.
III. Series: Interpersonal violence; v. 13.
RJ507.A29K37   1996
618.92′85822303—dc20   96-4425

This book is printed on acid-free paper.

97 98 99 10 9 8 7 6 5 4 3 2

Sage Production Editor: *Michèle Lingre*   Sage Typesetter: *Marion Warren*

Contents

PHASE I. Establishing Therapeutic Rapport

PHASE II. Exploration of Trauma

PHASE III. Repairing the Sense of Self

PHASE IV. Becoming Future Oriented

Foreword

As I supervise and consult with individuals who work with sexually abused children and adolescents, I hear many requests for specific treatment strategies. These requests are prompted by a number of factors that include the following: There is relatively little specific training offered in graduate programs about the treatment of sexually abused and traumatized children; therapists often feel overwhelmed when in the same room with a child or a group of children who have been traumatized; and successful therapy with children and adolescents who have difficulty talking about trauma oftentimes needs to be nonverbal and activity-based. I believe these factors were appreciated in the writing of this book.

One of the more exciting papers I have read recently describes the bind therapists are in when they use verbal, symbolic interventions to tackle nonverbal, symbolic representations (Santostefano & Calicchia, 1992). This type of representation is characteristic of the "unspeakable" aspects and experiences of abuse. The development of a therapeutic relationship creates an arena in which the nonverbal prescriptions for action, which characterize the fight or flight response to trauma, can emerge. Over time, the child can begin to verbalize his or her experiences and negotiate "an evolving set of meanings" (Santostefano & Calicchia, 1992, p. 665). The authors describe the need for a creative approach that appreciates the role of nonverbal, activity-based relationships in helping the child move forward.

At the same time, therapy with children must be more than a random collection of activities. The simple recitation of positive self-statements, or the writing down of "safety rules," are also insufficient approaches to facilitating enduring personal development. The attuned relationship is still the tree, and strategies are the ornaments.

I have known Dr. Karp for a number of years and know that she strives to practice in an empirically based and accountable manner. Consequently, I was not surprised when reading this book to realize that she and her coauthor have developed much more than a simple compendium of treatment strategies. A good, theory-driven case is made for the strategies that are outlined. I believe they can enhance therapeutic work with a broad range of children and adolescents.

In my recent book, *Psychotherapy With Sexually Abused Boys* (Friedrich, 1995), I outlined three broad theoretical considerations in the treatment of all sexually abused children. These reflect the phenomenon of *attachment* as being a central component in children's development in response to stress, the *disregulating* aspect of trauma, and the effect of trauma on the child's *sense of self*. With this bias in mind, I read through the treatment strategies that are outlined in this book.

Although Dr. Karp and Ms. Butler were not aware of the three-part model that I used in writing the above-mentioned book, the majority of the strategies that they outline fall into these three different domains. For example, the activities they describe in both Phases III and IV (i.e., repairing the sense of self and becoming future oriented) are directly related to a *sense of self*. I believe that this book's emphasis on disclosure of the trauma has direct relevance to the disregulating effect of unarticulated trauma.

The authors are also aware that trauma reflects a continuum of experiences. All therapists who use this book must also appreciate the diversity of abuse sequelae. Trauma also affects a continuum of children. Each of these children varies from the next in terms of the support they receive, their capacities to deal with distress, and their developmental maturity and coping styles.

Disclosure of trauma is a complex process. My thinking about disclosure certainly has evolved over my years in working with traumatized children. For example, I moved from an initial stance in which I was reluctant to be directive, to a second position in which I was vigorously directive, and finally, to the point I am at now, which is that disclosure can occur in many different ways and can be useful for some children but not others. The utility of disclosure to an individual child is more often a function not merely of the child, but of the child and his or her environment.

Disclosure of trauma also is related to Santostefano and Calicchia's (1992) paper. Severe trauma, experienced at an early age, may be encoded with minimal language elaboration. How then can it be helpful to have a child recite what happened to him or her? Furthermore, how is it possible for trauma to be fully disclosed in these cases? How does the language-based therapist help in these situations? You do so by creating a place where the nonverbal (e.g., instinctive grabbing of crotch when seeing a man) gradually can be made verbal (e.g., "he did something wrong to me") or symbolic (e.g., nurturing the doll whose "pooper" has an "owie").

This leads to an important point. There is no single way to treat such a diverse group of children. It is not the intention of this book to be simply a grab bag of "things to do when you're in a jam." The authors state that fact in a number of ways, but it certainly bears repeating.

Treating traumatized children is not something we need to leave to minimally prepared practitioners. Children live in a context in which they may or may not be supported. Bombarding them with a random collection of strategies that may or may not be sensitive to this context can be either helpful or nonhelpful. However, even the most experienced and seasoned therapist will meet children who can benefit from the treatment techniques that are outlined in this book.

I also appreciate the presentation of treatment phases. Again, children will chart their own course, but the phases outlined reflect child development, an ongoing process that characterizes all clinical therapy.

I know that both authors would be enormously gratified if, at some point in the future, individuals who had read this book had put a range of these strategies to an empirical test. It would be delightful to read that someone had determined, for example, that at the end of a developmentally and theoretically sound course of treatment, a combination of disclosure, addressing issues of self, and developing a more hopeful future had both immediate and delayed positive effects. This would reflect the mixture of clinical and empirical approaches that can move the field forward.

William N. Friedrich
Professor and Consultant
Mayo Clinic and Medical School

Acknowledgments

This book is the culmination of several years of working in the field of child maltreatment. Traci and I envisioned this book while working with a seven-year-old girl sent to our facility from out of state. This gave me a wonderful opportunity to see just how gifted Traci is in working with traumatized children. I owe her a debt of gratitude for her energy, vitality, and creativity in formulating ideas for many of the activities included in this book.

There are a number of colleagues and associates in private practice who have been supportive and encouraging. I would like to acknowledge them: Jean Baker, Rachel Burkholder, Joan Rosenblatt, Patricia Woolf, Margaret Ronstadt, and Larry Morris, who also was kind enough to share my work with C. Terry Hendrix. Without Larry's kind words this book may not have been published. My closest associate is Marta Ketchel. She and I meet weekly over lunch to keep our sanity. Sage Bergstrom works with me at Desert Hills in our Trauma Program. She has been instrumental in our program.

I would also like to acknowledge those in the field of trauma who have inspired me. First and foremost, John Briere, for his brilliance and moral support. Bill Friedrich has been both encouraging and thoughtful. I can't thank him enough for agreeing to write the Foreword for this book. I have also learned so much from others in the community network of "abuse" professionals—Diana Elliott, Eliana Gil, David Finkelhor, Lucy Berliner, Roland Summit, and Lenore Terr are just a few of those who I thank for their writings in this field. David Corwin holds a special spot for introducing me to the American Professional Society on the Abuse of Children (AP-SAC) in 1987. I have gained tremendously from this association.

Jon Conte was formidable in the organization of this book. With his guidance as our professional editor for the Interpersonal Violence Series, we went through many changes. It was his suggestion that we include Case Studies. I feel it was an important addition. At times I wondered if it would ever be done. It reminded me of seeing my major professor during the writing of my dissertation and leaving with more material to include—I began avoiding him. I must say though, I valued Jon's suggestions. They greatly enhanced the book. I also want to thank C. Terry Hendrix for believing in this book.

A special thanks is extended to my twin sister, Carol Silverander, for always being there for me. There were times during the writing of this book that she gave me strength to persevere. I also want to thank my sister, Nancy Davison, who was always there to listen and give feedback to the stories I wrote for this book. She is a gifted counselor and writer of children's stories.

Finally, my deepest gratitude goes to my husband and best friend, Len, for all his support and encouragement over the years, and for believing in me. He is truly an inspiration. His family law specialty gives him a certain connectedness to my field. I see him as a mentor as well as my soul mate. We have endured the loss of a child as well as the joy and turmoil of raising two sons. We have also gone through the agony and ecstasy of writing a book together. Words alone cannot express my appreciation to him.

Cheryl Karp

I would first like to acknowledge the courageous children who have trusted enough to share their experiences, thoughts, feelings and pain. I believe these children have been "teachers" and it is their bravery in moving from being victims of abuse to survivors which drives me to continue my work.

I also want to thank Cheryl Karp for "taking me under her wing," allowing me to realize one of my dreams and become an author. She also provided me with the opportunity to give back to the children and my colleagues in a meaningful way. If it were not for Cheryl's continual guidance, encouragement, perseverance and shared vision this project may not have been finished. A very special thanks to Len Karp for all the mashed potatoes on Sundays!

Lastly, I would like to thank my family and friends for all of the support and encouragement over the last two and a half years. Renie, I am grateful for all of the unconditional love and support. To my parents, I am thankful for the belief and support that I can follow any dream and achieve anything I choose. To my friends, Kirsten, Pattie, Kathy, Michael, Carol, Betty and the many others who continually asked about our book, gave encouragement in its worth and gave me the message that this could be more than just a dream—thank you. A special thanks is extended to Kristin Gauthier for her superb artwork. We owe a lot to her for creating our little people for the activity book. Her artwork makes the activity book inviting.

Traci Butler

Introduction and Theory

Anyone who has worked with abused children knows the struggles and frustrations of trying to help kids emerge from their experiences of trauma to become healthy survivors. We have experienced similar struggles and frustrations as we searched the libraries and bookstores for materials to help us in our work with abused children.

We are both currently on staff in a psychiatric center for youth and their families. The center provides treatment for abused children from 2 years old, in the Early Childhood Program, through adolescence, in our older child and adolescent programs. This is a fairly extensive age range, and what we have discovered is that although a variety of materials is available for adult survivors, limited resources are available for children.

One day over lunch we were discussing a mutual 7-year-old patient, who was severely traumatized by multiple perpetrators, and sharing our frustrations with the paucity of child-oriented materials to address her victimization. We began brainstorming . . . . How do we get her to start processing her abuse history? What "hands-on" activities will be nonthreatening enough to get her to open up yet allow her to safely deal with the specifics? Besides the use of a journal, what else could we create that would allow her to work through her abuse and be something tangible to keep for years to come?

At this point we decided our book should be directed to all children of trauma (Briere, 1992; Finkelhor & Associates, 1986). For the purposes of this book, we are defining *trauma* as the psychological effects suffered from sexual, physical, and/or emotional abuse. Interestingly, child abuse has been recognized as a significant social problem only in the past few decades.

In our research on this devastating problem, we found the report prepared by the National Center on Child Abuse Prevention Research (Wiese & Daro, 1995) to be quite disturbing. This report revealed that 3,140,000 children were reported to Child Protective Services (CPS) agencies as victims of child maltreatment in 1994. Overall, child abuse reports have maintained a steady growth since 1989, with an average increase of about 5% each year.

Our purpose in creating this book is to provide children who have been abused or neglected with a tangible, activity-oriented means to work through the various phases of recovery from the abuse they have suffered, much like Bass and Davis (1988) have done in their book for adult survivors of child sexual abuse. Also included in each chapter are actual case examples and a "walk-through" of just how the activities can be applied. It is our hope that they further facilitate use of the activities by the therapist.

This book is *not* intended to assess whether a child has been abused. We can only assume that a thorough assessment has been completed and that children who are victims of abuse will benefit from these strategies. We have included an interview schedule, the Child Abuse Trauma Interview (CATI), that we have devised to assess the extent of the child's abuse history (see the Appendix in the Activity Book). We have borrowed some ideas for this from Briere's (1992) Child Maltreatment Interview Schedule, which is for adult survivors of child maltreatment.

Many other excellent resources review assessment of children suspected of being maltreated (Achenback, 1991; American Professional Society on the Abuse of Children [APSAC], 1995; Briere, 1989;

Finkelhor & Associates, 1986; Garbarino, Guttman, & Seeley, 1986; Gil, 1991; Gil & Johnson, 1993; Helfer & Kempe, 1987; Karp & Karp, 1989; MacFarlane et al., 1986).

The first chapter of this book focuses on a brief review of child sexual development and how this is disrupted by trauma. With the focus in society shifting to "abnormal" behaviors of children, we are often asked, "What is normal?" In this chapter, we have included a review of normal sexual development. We also include "red flags" of abnormal sexual behaviors.

Our hope is that traumatized children will find the activities provided in this book a safe way to explore abusive experiences. The end goal of this project is to assist the child in moving from being a victim of abuse to becoming a healthier survivor. We believe this process is accomplished through providing *corrective* and *reparative* experiences, as Eliana Gil (1991) has so aptly stated in her book *The Healing Power of Play: Therapy With Abused Children.*

According to Gil (1991), a corrective approach provides the child with experiences within a safe and trusting environment that enable the child to gain a sense of safety, trust, and an enhanced sense of self. The reparative aspect of treatment is designed to assist the child in processing the traumatic event(s), allowing the child to understand and incorporate the experience(s) in a healthier manner.

Finkelhor and Browne (1986) have proposed a model of analyzing the effects of trauma in terms of four trauma-causing factors that they refer to as *traumagenic dynamics.* Although they refer to these in their discussion of the effects of sexual abuse, they also identify them as generalized dynamics associated with other kinds of trauma.

The four traumagenic dynamics are traumatic sexualization, stigmatization, betrayal, and powerlessness. According to Finkelhor and Browne (1986), "these dynamics, when present, alter the child's cognitive and emotional orientation to the world, and create trauma by distorting a child's self-concept, world view, and affective capacities" (pp. 180-181).

Another important aspect of child abuse trauma is covered by Briere (1989, 1992) in his explanation of the *abuse dichotomy.* Negative self-evaluation may arise from the victim's attempt to make sense of his or her abusive experiences. This process can eventually lead to the child's perceptions that he or she is inherently bad and therefore deserved the abuse.

According to Briere (1992), the series of quasilogical inferences, characterized by the child's dichotomous thinking and egocentricity, appears to proceed as follows:

1. I am being hurt, emotionally or physically, by a parent or other trusted adult.
2. Based on how I think about the world thus far, this injury can only be due to one of two things: either I am bad or my parent is (the abuse dichotomy).
3. I have been taught by other adults, either at home or in school, that parents are always right, and always do things for your own good (any other alternative is very frightening). When they occasionally hurt you, it is for your own good, because you have been bad. This is called punishment.
4. Therefore, it must be my fault that I am being hurt, just as my parent says. This must be punishment. I must deserve this.
5. Therefore, I am as bad as whatever is done to me (the punishment must fit the crime: anything else suggests parental badness, which I have rejected). I am bad because I have been hurt. I have been hurt because I am bad.
6. I am hurt quite often, and/or quite deeply, therefore I must be very bad. (p. 28)

The abuse dichotomy can lead to cognitive distortions that persist well into adulthood. This unhealthy thought process can lead to self-deprecating conclusions about one's self-worth. Experts in the field of child maltreatment agree that cognitive distortions, created by physical, sexual, and psychological abuse, have devastating, lifelong effects if left untreated (Briere, 1992; Finkelhor & Browne, 1986; Gil, 1991).

The *Diagnostic and Statistical Manual of Mental Disorders—Fourth Edition* (*DSM-IV*) (1994) lists diagnostic criteria for Posttraumatic Stress Disorder (PTSD), the diagnosis most closely associated with victims of interpersonal violence, such as torture, rape, physical assault, and child abuse.

The *DSM-IV* was revised recently to include specific symptoms attributed to children who suffer from PTSD. In general, to receive a diagnosis of PTSD, a person must have been exposed to a traumatic event in which

> (1) the person experienced, witnessed, or was confronted with an event or events that involved actual or threatened death or serious injury, or a threat to the physical integrity of self or others, and (2) the person's response involved intense fear, helplessness, or horror. *Note:* In children, this may be expressed instead by disorganized or agitated behavior. (pp. 427-428)

In addition to the above symptoms, the person must meet several other criteria that have persisted for more than a month and have caused clinically significant distress or impairment:

- The traumatic event is persistently reexperienced by young children through repetitive play in which themes or aspects of the trauma are expressed, frightening dreams recur, trauma-specific reenactment may occur, and intense psychological distress and/or physiological reactivity when cues that symbolize or resemble an aspect of the traumatic event occur.
- The child experiences persistent avoidance of things associated with the trauma and numbing of general responsiveness.
- The child has persistent symptoms of increased arousal such as difficulty falling or staying asleep, irritability or outbursts of anger, difficulty concentrating, hypervigilance, or exaggerated startle response. (*DSM-IV*, 1994, pp. 427-429)

Most studies that examine posttraumatic stress in child abuse focus on sexual and physical abuse. When PTSD is associated with psychological abuse, children generally have been "terrorized" or have witnessed violent assaults on others (Briere, 1992; Terr, 1990).

The *Practice Guidelines* for psychological maltreatment, prepared by APSAC (1995), include six forms of psychological maltreatment: (a) spurning, (b) terrorizing, (c) isolating, (d) exploiting or corrupting, (e) denying emotional responsiveness, and (f) unwarranted denial of mental health care, medical care, or education.

According to the *Practice Guidelines*, a repeated pattern or extreme incident(s) of the above conditions constitute psychological maltreatment. It conveys a message that the child is "worthless, flawed, unloved, endangered, or only valuable in meeting someone else's needs" (APSAC, 1995, p. 7).

In reviewing the effects of abuse, it is important to address various factors that result in an increase in trauma. Briere (1992) mentions several studies that have addressed certain characteristics that are associated with greater trauma than abuse without such characteristics: greater duration and frequency of the abuse (Elliott & Briere, 1992), multiple perpetrators (Peters, 1988), presence of penetration or intercourse (Finkelhor, Hotaling, Lewis, & Smith, 1989), physically forced sexual contact (Fromuth, 1986), abuse at an earlier age (Zivney, Nash, & Hulsey, 1988), concurrent physical abuse (Briere & Runtz, 1989), and victim feelings of powerlessness, betrayal, and/or stigma at the time of the abuse (Henschel, Briere, Magallanes, & Smiljanich, 1990).

The above studies emphasize the need to address the impact of abuse from various perspectives. The child abuse victim often has suffered many of the abusive experiences that are listed above. It is not unusual that a child who has been physically and sexually abused also has suffered psychological torture. Many children have been abused at a very young age through physical force and made to feel powerless and betrayed by the perpetrator.

❏ Abuse-Focused Psychotherapy

We have used a framework based on abuse-focused psychotherapy to address all aspects of child maltreatment. As Briere (1992) so aptly stressed in *Child Abuse Trauma: Theory and Treatment of the Lasting Effects*, the message conveyed to adult survivors of child maltreatment when using abuse-focused psychotherapy is to acknowledge the struggle to survive the child maltreatment. He also stresses the need to reframe the coping behaviors that are often seen as sick or "dysfunctional" as being a healthy accommodation to the toxic environment.

Abuse-focused psychotherapy for children, as it is for adults, is not about a cure—it is about survival. The child's work is to gain the courage to go back to the frightening thoughts and images of the trauma and explore them in a safer environment where there is a better sense of control. The child must then gain the skills necessary to cope with what may be seen as a frightening world in which to grow up as a healthier adult.

The therapist's job is to create an environment in which the child can do this important work in a safe, nurturing, and protective setting. Unless the child feels safe and protected, he or she most likely will not engage in this process of healing. Therefore, setting the stage for a healthy therapeutic bond is an important aspect of the healing process.

In approaching the child victim of abuse, we have used a phenomenological therapeutic stance and the premise of self-psychology theory as the underpinning of abuse-focused psychotherapy. Phenomenology is a theory that behavior is determined by the survivor's personal experiences and perceptions rather than by reality, because it can be described in physical, objective terms.

Self-psychology is based on the theories offered by Kohut and colleagues (Elson, 1987; Kohut, 1971, 1977), which focuses on the emergence of the self. Although the "self" is yet to be determined clearly (Briere, 1992; Stern, 1985), Stern (1985) points out an important observation:

> Even though the nature of self may forever elude the behavioral sciences, the sense of self stands as an important subjective reality, a reliable, evident phenomenon that the sciences cannot dismiss. How we experience ourselves in relation to others provides a basic organizing perspective for all interpersonal events. (p. 6)

Briere (1992) notes that severe child maltreatment may interfere with the child's *access* to a sense of self. This creates a situation in which the child is prone to identity confusion, boundary issues, and feelings of personal emptiness. Self-psychology theory stresses the importance of empathy and mastery in the formation of self-esteem. It is rooted deeply in child development.

In working with child victims of maltreatment, we believe it is important to be empathic and child focused. The child's behaviors and feelings need to be addressed from his or her perspective in order to understand the meaning and impact the abuse has created for the child.

In some of the activities, we have used cognitive-behavioral techniques, such as cognitive restructuring, to assist the child in challenging his or her distorted perceptions. This provides important tools in the child's struggle toward developing a healthier sense of self.

In the following section, we have addressed what we see as specific phases in the recovery process.

❏ Phases of the Recovery Process

Taking into account the dynamics of trauma, the reparative process, and the individual needs of each child, we see the general phases of recovery as being four-pronged. In the first phase, the therapist must build a positive therapeutic relationship with the child. This is accomplished by providing a safe and nurturing environment that is hoped to encourage a sense of trust.

The goal in Chapters 2 through 4 will focus on the first phase of recovery. The activities are designed to be less threatening and to encourage the child to begin building therapeutic rapport, identifying feelings, and exploring boundaries without focusing specifically on the trauma. It is important to note that traumatized children have an impaired ability to trust others and typically have difficulties with appropriate boundaries.

Abused children often have impaired abilities to judge the trustworthiness of others and will often mistrust as well as distrust others. In other words, some children will have loose boundaries and give "blanket trust," while others will not trust anyone. Establishing trust and boundaries is an important aspect of trauma resolution. There is no set time on how long this process may take. In our opinion, trauma resolution is not typically conducive to short-term therapy. It is important to go at a pace specific to the needs of each child. If the first phase is not well established, there is potential to retraumatize the child by moving into the reparative phase prematurely.

The second phase of recovery is the exploration of various aspects of the trauma, which incorporates both of Gil's goals of treatment—

the corrective and reparative experiences of the child. This is the abuse-focused aspect of treatment. The second phase, Chapters 5 through 7, includes identifying specific people and places that feel unsafe to the child as well as "secrets," memories, nightmares, and "monsters" associated with traumatic experiences. This can be an extremely difficult and time-consuming process in the child's therapy. As the child starts recalling the trauma, you may find yourself back at the beginning stages of therapy.

The child's foundation of trust may begin to crumble as he or she recalls specific aspects of the traumatic experience(s), which may result in projecting distrust onto you as the therapist. It has been our experience in working with young children that many times they are not at a cognitive level that allows them to distinguish between prior experiences and current reality. For example, a therapist may tell the child that he or she will have a "special relationship" that is safe to share secrets. The child may interpret this to be similar to the "special," "secret" relationship that was shared with the abuser. This can foster all sorts of fears that can undermine the foundation of trust that previously had been built. If this occurs, you will need to go back to safer, rapport-building activities.

The third phase of the recovery process, covered in Chapters 8 and 9, is repairing the sense of self. This includes processing various aspects associated with guilt and shame stemming from the trauma, working through the *stuck* feelings, and developing appropriate skills to cope with ongoing feelings.

Guilt and shame are often so entrenched in the child's sense of self that it is often difficult to let go of these unhealthy beliefs completely. It is hoped that the activities in this book will help the child begin to address this difficult phase of recovery, leading to a sense of mastery, increased control, and an ability to trust.

To us, guilt and shame are at the core of the damage done by abusive experiences, leading to seriously impaired self-esteem. Reparation of the self can become a lifelong process, even when aspects of the trauma have been resolved.

The final phase, as we see it, is assisting the child in becoming more future oriented. As the child explores the long journey of his or her own recovery, it is important to look not only at the here and now and all of the accomplishments achieved thus far but also toward the future. Chapter 10 is designed not only to review the child's accomplishments thus far but also will assist the child in setting future goals.

Throughout the process of trauma resolution, the child is so identified with the *victim role* that it can be difficult to move from the helplessness associated with abuse to a sense of empowerment and control. We strongly believe that it is critical to assist the child in the learning skills necessary to deal with the here and now as well as setting goals for the future. It is hoped that the child will emerge into a healthier survivor rather than remain a victim of his or her past.

❏ Therapist Issues

We have found through our own work with abused children that there are a myriad of feelings that you, as the therapist, will experience while working with abused children, especially as children begin to work through the abuse histories. You need to be aware of them and expect them.

When working with abused children, it is best for therapists with abuse histories to have worked through their own traumas to a large degree. Periodically, it may be necessary to reenter your own therapy so that issues elicited by an abused child do not interfere with the child's therapy.

You may find it personally overwhelming as you walk through the pain with the child while working through this phase of recovery. We found that having a colleague to confide in and process through the emotional aspects of each case has enhanced our therapeutic effectiveness, and it has helped us keep a healthier perspective.

Various warning signs may alert you to the possibility that therapeutic boundaries may be an issue. You may find yourself feeling sorry for the child and needing to rescue him or her from the abusive experiences. This is not establishing healthy boundaries.

You also may find yourself angry at a particular child for taking advantage of your nurturing when in essence your relationship has become too enmeshed. This unhealthy relationship can manifest itself in various behaviors exhibited by the child, from demanding constant attention to venting anger at you with assaultive actions, such as hitting, kicking, biting, punching, and/or yelling.

The psychodynamic concept of *transference* is applicable when working with abused children. The child transfers the thoughts and feelings about a primary person in his or her life onto a safer adult, the therapist. In turn, the therapist may then react to the child's behavior in a *countertransference* manner, often resulting in hostile feelings.

This process of transference and countertransference underscores the need to discuss and work through your feelings with a colleague. This work is difficult and emotionally provoking. Thus there is a need to ensure clear boundaries to provide the appropriate treatment needed.

This book has been designed to delve much deeper into an explanation of each phase of the healing process as each chapter is introduced. The introductions are followed by detailed instructions of how each activity is organized as well as an explanation for each activity.

Case studies have been included in each chapter to assist the understanding of how some of the activities have been used in actual therapy situations. We have given a brief case history, an example of the dialogue between the therapist and the child during the activity, as well as clinical impressions of the child's work. We have also included some drawings made by the children in the course of some of their therapy sessions. Names, characteristics, and circumstances have been altered in order to protect the children's identity.

Many activities are provided in each chapter, so the therapist may pick and choose which activities will assist in the child's therapy. It is not necessary to complete all the activities in this book. It is up to you, as the child's therapist, to decide which activities will be most beneficial to the child. We have outlined the age range recommended for each activity.

As stated previously, the chapters have been organized to proceed through the healing process; however, each child enters therapy at a different stage in his or her own recovery. Therefore, certain chapters or activities may not seem needed or specific to a particular child's issues. Again, it is up to you to decide which chapters and activities will assist you in your therapy goals.

Please note: These activities are not designed to be given to children indiscriminately or without therapeutic supervision and processing of each activity. The activities also are not to be regarded as the only form of therapy. Children need to engage in ongoing dialogue about their feelings, and some children will need play therapy as their primary form of treatment. These activities can be an adjunct to other forms of therapeutic intervention.

It is important to remember that a child should never be forced to engage in an activity unwillingly. Pressuring the child may retraumatize the already traumatized child. This may alert you to the need to concentrate on the less abuse-focused activities found in Chapters 2 through 4. We hope this will assist you in your therapy with abused children.

1

Overview of Child Sexual Development

To understand and appreciate the devastating effects sexual abuse has on children, it is best to first review normal child sexual development. As children progress from infancy to adulthood, they move through dynamic and ever-changing periods. What happens during this process has a critical effect on future functioning. People who interact with the child during these critical years surely will have a significant impact on later development through the life span (Helfer, 1987).

There has been a concerted effort in the past decade to educate therapists and parents about the "red flags" associated with child sexual abuse. In this effort, we have often neglected to educate others about what constitutes normal sexual development. Professionals also are confronted with what is age-appropriate "sex play" between children and when child sexual behavior is abusive.

As stated earlier, sexual development occurs in progressive stages similar to psychosocial and cognitive development. Cultural norms come into play when evaluating what is normal versus abnormal sexual development. According to Martinson (1991),

> Each child's development will be markedly influenced by the cultural norms and expectations, familial interactions and values, and the interpersonal experiences encountered. . . . Organic capacities, cognitive development and integration, and intrapsychic influences further determine the rate and extent of development of the sexual capacity. (p. 58)

❏ Stages of Sexual Development

PRESCHOOL CHILDREN (0-4 YEARS)

Children at this stage have intense curiosity about the world around them and about their bodies. Genital play or masturbation normally begins in the first year of life and continues throughout the preschool years as a self-soothing behavior. At this stage, children generally are not discreet and masturbate in front of others. Self-exploration and self-stimulation are random and sporadic (Cunningham & MacFarlane, 1991).

Children in this age group tend to "discover" that when certain parts of the body are touched, poked, rubbed, or otherwise stimulated, pleasant sensations occur. As in other aspects of their life, when something pleasurable occurs, children usually seek to repeat the event. Actual rhythmic manipulation with the hand does not appear to occur until children are approximately 2½ to 3 years of age, when small muscle control is developed sufficiently.

Parents or caretakers provide a positive or negative reinforcement according to how they react to children's self-exploration. For example, if the caretaker hits the child's hands or genitals when self-exploration occurs, it is less likely to recur. The child will make a negative association between self-touching and pain. On the other hand, if the parent allows the self-exploration while continuing to change the diaper and does not punish the child, a positive or neutral association is made between self-exploration and the diapering circumstance (Gil & Johnson, 1993).

According to Martinson (1991), from birth on children have occasional erections or vaginal secretions, and by age 5 any child is capable of autoerotic experiences. It is also common for this age group to be interested in looking at or poking others' bodies. They also may try sticking fingers or other small objects into openings in the body, such as noses, ears, belly buttons, eyes, mouths, or genitals. They are very exploratory. Young children who sit on women's laps may be observed to poke or squeeze what they call "boobies." This is done in fun and they will often laugh or run away with delight.

Children ages 2 and 3 are especially interested in the bathroom activity of others. It is not uncommon to find preschoolers walking into the bathroom to see what others are doing. They may use an inordinate number of bathroom words, such as "poo-poo" or "caca." They also may learn slang words for body parts and then will use these words relentlessly, often to the dismay of concerned parents or caretakers.

Preschoolers will take advantage of opportunities to touch others' genitalia if permitted or allowed to. However, they take redirection quickly and respond positively to limit setting about touching others' bodies. This touching is of an exploratory rather than a coercive nature.

It is common to watch 3- to 4-year-olds "play house" by pretending to be mommy or daddy. They also may have the mother and father dolls kiss, lie in bed together, make babies, and have arguments (Gil & Johnson, 1993). This is mostly imitative behavior. It is noteworthy that children will imitate only what they have observed (in life or from television).

Young children also like to play "doctor." However, when they give examinations, they are unlikely to include a pelvic examination. In this day and age, temperatures usually are taken with a digital thermometer in the mouth or under the arm. But it still may be imitative to try inserting a play thermometer in the rectum if they have watched this on television or have seen this in a book.

Abnormal sexual behavior occurs when curiosity becomes an obsessive preoccupation, when exploration becomes a reenactment of specific adult sexual activity, or when children's behavior involves coercion toward others or injury to themselves (Cunningham & MacFarlane, 1991). As previously stated, sexual play is part of preschoolers' curiosity about the world around them as well as about their own body parts.

YOUNG SCHOOL-AGE CHILDREN (5-7 YEARS)

Young school-age children continue to touch and fondle their own genitals, evolving into masturbation. At this stage of development, they become more secretive about their self-touching, and they may begin to masturbate in a less random way. They have discovered creative ways of masturbating and may repeat them. As stated previously, this is usually done in private rather than in public.

Young girls often discover that if they lift their vagina to the water spout in the bathtub, the water stimulation feels good. They may then share this new information with girlfriends. Similarly, young boys may discover that climbing or shimmying poles feels good on their penis, and they may increase the frequency of this behavior (Gil & Johnson, 1993).

Interest in viewing others' bodies continues, although it changes from curiosity seeking to game playing. Games such as "I'll show you mine, you show me yours" begin at this developmental stage, and "doctor" continues to be a fun game. During this time children become extremely interested in sex words and dirty jokes, often not fully understanding the punch lines.

Children in this age group watch and ask questions, such as "Where did I come from?" They are interested in pictures of the human body and may giggle a great deal when they see people kissing on TV. It is common to say they are "grossed out" by displays of affection but are fascinated by it at the same time.

Feelings of needing privacy emerge at this age. Children may start draping towels around their bodies and demand that parents, siblings, or caretakers knock on their doors before entering.

Depending on regional and/or cultural differences, some children in this age group begin to date, although this is usually done in groups (Gil & Johnson, 1993). Some young children may hold hands and kiss.

Abnormal sexual behavior at this stage of development would be sexual penetration, genital kissing or oral copulation, and simulated intercourse (Cunningham & MacFarlane, 1991).

LATENCY-AGED CHILDREN (7-12 YEARS)

Latency-aged children have a range of sexual interests. They continue to have peer contact in school, may begin to experiment with sexual behaviors, and may have alternating periods of disinhibition and inhibition.

Children in this age group vary a great deal. During this time frame most children enter puberty. Boys may develop pubic hair and the ability to masturbate to ejaculation, and girls may develop pubic hair, breasts, and begin their menses. Both boys and girls can have a growth spurt during this period, and physiological changes are imminent.

This age group has active hormonal changes that create a wide range of physical and emotional sensations. They may give more time to masturbatory activities than their younger counterparts. Some children in this age group become exhibitionistic (Gil & Johnson, 1993).

At ages 9 and 10, children begin seeking information about sex and look for books and diagrams that explain their own organs and functions. Swearing begins during this stage. Touching others' genitalia usually takes place in a gamelike atmosphere and involves stroking or rubbing (Cunningham & MacFarlane, 1991).

Latency-aged boys develop a certain locker room behavior in which they are often nude, and they may slap one another on the buttocks and tell dirty jokes. Ejaculation contests may occur. These boys also start comparing penis size. Girls, on the other hand, also have locker room behavior that may include comparing breast sizes and experimenting with varying degrees of nudity.

Developmentally, preadolescents (ages 10-12) are focused on establishing relationships with peers. Many preadolescents, and certainly adolescents, engage in sexual activity with peers, including open-mouth kissing, sexual fondling, simulated intercourse, sexual penetration behaviors, and intercourse. Preadolescents find themselves falling in love.

According to Friedrich (1990), older children are likely to assume cultural norms and restraints. Due to all the moral, religious, and health restrictions on sexuality, many children avoid penile or genital contact and engage in cunnilingus and fellatio. Other children fear and/or avoid sexual contact until much later.

Although most of these experiences are heterosexual, it is common for preadolescents and adolescents to have some same-gender sexual experiences. During this stage there may be intense interest in viewing others' bodies, especially members of the opposite sex. This may take the form of looking at photographs or published material, including pornography.

Abnormal sexual behavior for preadolescents and adolescents would include sexual play with younger children as well as coercive, exploitive, or aggressive sex with same-age peers (Sgroi, 1988).

❏ Children's Sexual Behavior Problems

Regardless of a child's age, abusive sexual behavior is considered abnormal. In its preliminary report (National Adolescent Perpetrator Network, 1988), the Task Force on Juvenile Sexual Offending stated,

> Sexual interactions involving children with peers or younger children are problematic if the relationship is coercive, exploitive or aggressive or threatens the physical or psychological well-being of either participant. . . . The exploitive nature of child sexual offending is measured in terms of size and age differential; power or authority differential; lack of equality and consent; and threats, violence or aggression." (p. 42)

Sgroi (1988) uses similar criteria in suggesting that answers to the following questions indicate whether a sexual activity may be considered abusive:

- What are the power positions of the participants?
- Is force or intimidation used?
- Is ritual or sadistic abuse involved?

- Is secrecy involved?
- How developmentally appropriate are the sexual acts?

Johnson (Gil & Johnson, 1993) has devised a continuum of sexual disturbance for children 12 and under who have intact reality testing and are not considered developmentally delayed. Johnson has divided these children into four groups. Group I includes children who engage in *Normal Childhood Sexual Exploration*, Group II comprises *Sexually Reactive Children*, Group III includes *Children With Extensive Mutual Sexual Behaviors*, and Group IV includes *Children Who Molest Other Children*.

If you spend much time working with sexually abused children, you may want to read more about these four groups. It has been our experience that sexually abused children often gravitate to one another and may engage in behaviors consistent with the last three groups mentioned above. To effectively treat and provide comprehensive therapeutic care for these children, one must have a clear understanding of each group and the behaviors consistent with each group.

❏ Parental Guidance

Probably one of the most critical factors in child sexual development is the level of parental guidance. Parents play an important role in providing values about sexuality to their children. According to Gil and Johnson (1993), when parents view sex as dirty, inappropriate, or secretive, they may set rigid and restrictive limits on healthy curiosity, self-exploration, and questions. When children are punished, chastised, or humiliated for appropriate sexual exploration, they may begin to associate sex with shame or guilt.

Some parents may be oversexualized, creating a sexualized environment. Although it may not always be sexualized behavior, adult nudity or lack of appropriate boundaries can have a detrimental effect on a child's sexuality. Other parents may be undersexualized, creating an environment in which sex is taboo. Households in which children never see parents behaving affectionately render a child naive about appropriate displays of affection. Either polarity can negatively affect the child's healthy sexual development.

Children need an open environment in which they can ask questions and learn about sexuality. We all know that if children cannot find the answers at home, they will turn to their peer group or their own experimentation for answers.

PHASE I

*Establishing
Therapeutic Rapport*

Who Am I? Image Building, Goal Setting, and Therapeutic Trust

Developing rapport and building a therapeutic alliance with the abused or traumatized child is an important goal early in the therapeutic relationship (Haugaard & Reppucci, 1988, pp. 237-238). Because most children don't seek out a therapist, it can be a difficult task. They may feel, as they have in the past, that decisions have been made for them.

Therapy may be seen as another adult forming a "secret" relationship with them, which, in the past, has led to their victimization. For emotionally and/or physically abused children, the therapist may symbolize the "punisher" due to the nature of the adult-child relationship. Therefore, it is important to give plenty of time for this rapport to develop. It is also important to understand the damage that resulted from the child's abusive history.

Children who have been abused, either sexually, physically or emotionally, experience severe damage to their self-esteem. Their sense of self is fragmented and often filled with self-hate, guilt, and confusion. The defense against these horrible emotions is to suppress them by pushing the feelings down deep inside or to act them out.

The abused child often will rely on unhealthy coping mechanisms such as dissociation, denial, or anger to defend against the overwhelming emotions that cannot be understood at such a young age. Dissociation allows the child to separate or split off from the emotional feelings, providing a sense of protection from difficult experiences. *DSM-IV* (1994) defines dissociation as "a disruption in the usual integrated functions of consciousness, memory, identity, or perception of the environment. The disturbance may be sudden or gradual, transient or chronic" (p. 477).

It is important to have a basic understanding of dissociation because many traumatized children do exhibit symptoms associated with this disorder, and this may interfere with the rapport-building phase of therapy. Gil (Gil & Johnson, 1993) refers to abused children as often reporting feelings of depersonalization and psychogenic amnesia for prior events. You may see this as a child just "staring off" or "spacing out." Children who dissociate will be unable to hear, process, or understand what is being discussed in either group or individual therapy. Therefore, it is important to assess this if you suspect that a child is not attentive and could be dissociative.

Developing a common language to "cue" children about their dissociative states can be helpful. It is important to point out to the child that this was a "survival" skill that worked very well for him or her at one time but is not so helpful now. The goal is to help the child gain a sense of mastery over this coping skill.

You may find as your therapeutic rapport grows stronger with the child that he or she may be more willing to share what is going on internally. This will allow you, as the therapist, to find better ways to cue the child and will encourage the child to be part of that process.

As stated earlier, the abused child also may use denial and/or anger to cope with traumatic experiences. A child who is in a state of denial may refuse to admit that anything has occurred. This child needs to see everything as "normal." This state of denial not only helps protect the people he or she loves but allows the child to keep the experiences at a distance.

The acting-out child, as the child who is dissociative or in denial, may be suffering from Posttraumatic Stress Disorder. This child may be acting out the violent experiences or is feeling so confused and turmoiled inside that he or she may be responding to internal chaos. These children are frequently labeled as having Oppositional Defiant or Attention-Deficit/Hyperactivity Disorder. Although their behaviors may be consistent with these disorders, it is also possible that the effects of the trauma have resulted in this display of behavior. Therefore, it is important to use caution when labeling abused children.

Traumatized children frequently feel out of control and powerless. They are not clear on just who they are. There is typically no trust in others, especially if the child experienced trauma in the first 5 years of life, causing disrupted ability to form attachments.

Traumatized children also may turn to various maladaptive means of coping with their own internal chaos. Overeating is just one of the behaviors used to numb the feelings of rage, shame, or despair, or is their only form of nurturance. Therefore, the way children see themselves is a good barometer of where they are in recovery.

Typically, the traumatized child struggles with so many issues that developing relationships is a difficult and time-consuming process. Therefore, building a solid foundation of trust is paramount. This chapter is designed to begin building rapport with the child in nonthreatening ways. The exercises will focus on helping children explore their own image as well as how they see themselves in relation to others.

The abused child often has a fragmented sense of self. The hope is that the child will build a rapport with you as the therapist so that he or she will be able to move through the more painful aspects of trauma recovery. The process becomes one of starting from the ground floor and rebuilding the child's sense of self.

The following activities are designed to assist children in exploring who they are in relation to their family and to begin working on individual goal setting. As the therapist working with the child, you are free to select the activities that seem to best facilitate the child's growth. However, we have organized the activities in a way we think follows a logical progression to address therapeutic needs.

A few case studies have been included to assist you in further understanding how some of these activities have been used in actual therapy situations. We have given a brief case history, an example of dialogue between the therapist and child during the activity, and clinical impressions.

If you find the child you are working with is extremely resistant, you may also want to supplement the activities listed with some of your own in an effort to meet individual therapeutic needs. We realize some children may need additional time on any given therapeutic goal in their treatment process.

As you work through the activities in this chapter with the child, you are building the therapeutic foundation necessary to process through more difficult stages of healing, which will be addressed in later chapters. It is unlikely that a child will experience a high level of stress when involved with the activities in this chapter. However, if the child you are working with does exhibit evidence of distress, proceed slowly and cautiously through the activities.

It is important to engage in a thorough processing of children's thoughts and feelings as they move forward. At the end of several of the activities listed in this manual you will find a section called "Processing." The "Processing" section is general. You most likely will add your own ideas as you get to know the child.

The Activity Book includes a section titled "Message to the Kids." You may want to read this to the child you are working with or give it to him or her to read. It is helpful to give the child a notebook to help organize the worksheets. At the completion of the therapy, the child will have lots of concrete memories of the work that has been completed.

❏ **Activity #1: All About Me!**

Objective: To build therapeutic rapport with the child.

This activity is designed to get your relationship started with the child. We have included factual questions for you to ask the child. This activity accomplishes two goals in building a therapeutic relationship. First, it provides additional information about the child.

Second, it is a nonthreatening means to begin the process of rapport building and communication with the child.

If you have additional questions that you want to include, feel free to add them to the inventory on a separate piece of paper. The more you can engage the child in a direct dialogue over nonthreatening material, the better the therapeutic bond becomes. This makes it much easier when you get to more difficult material later in the child's therapy.

Ages: Children between ages 6 and 12 should be able to respond to all of the questions in this activity. Most children from ages 9 to 12 will be able to complete this activity on their own. Younger children and/or children who have difficulties reading or writing may need you to read the inventory and act as a secretary.

Materials Needed: Activity sheet and pencil.

Instructions: Instruct the child to fill in the blank spaces provided on the inventory. If the child is unable to complete this on his or her own, you may act as the child's personal secretary, writing down what the child tells you.

If the child completes this on his or her own, you will need to go over the inventory together. This provides a nice opportunity to engage in positive dialogue.

Note: Prior to beginning this activity, an assessment of the child's reading and writing skills is important. It would be counter-therapeutic to give children a task that is beyond their functioning level, as they will become too frustrated with the activity and your requests. Assessment of children's functioning level can be done by asking their parents or informally by reading a book together.

Processing: Once the child is finished, review his or her answers. While reviewing the answers, you will want to ask additional questions, such as "Do you like your name?" "Tell me, what's the best/worst thing about your school?" "What makes him or her your best friend?" The important thing to remember in completing this activity is that the goal is to establish rapport. The more you can engage with the child and the more the child engages with you, the stronger the therapeutic bond.

❏ **Activity #2: Me!**

Objective: To assist the child in becoming more aware of how he or she views himself or herself.

This activity is designed to help you assess how the child sees himself or herself and to help in the assessment of the child's level of emotional maturity. Many times, traumatized children's pictures depict a regressed image.

Malchiodi (1990) discusses commonalities in artwork among abused children in her book *Breaking the Silence: Art Therapy With Children From Violent Homes.* These include sexual connotation, heads without bodies or bodies without the lower half, disorganization of body parts, encapsulation of a person, use of the color red and of a complementary color scheme, use of heart-shaped imagery, artistic regression, circles and wedges, and self-deprecation. Her study focused on children in women's shelters who had been sexually abused.

In her work with abused children, Gil (1992) cites several observations of drawings by abused children: startled eyes, open mouth, displacement of parts of the body, layering of colors (not just shading), body encased in something, signs of injury ("symbol of injury"), open cavities, and splitting or dissociation (e.g., picture of the child's spirit leaving the body).

Ages: This activity is designed for children ages 6 to 12 years. The younger or more emotionally immature or damaged child will have less details. The older, more mature child may be very detailed with his or her self-portrait.

Materials Needed: Sheet of paper and pencils, crayons, and/or markers.

Instructions: Instruct the child to draw a picture of himself or herself as complete as possible. You may need to provide encouragement or ask questions to facilitate this activity. For example, you might want to inquire whether the child has drawn all of himself or herself or whether the child wants to include more. Refrain from pointing out missing details or telling the child what to include in the self-portrait because these become your indicators of how the child views himself or herself.

Note: Regardless of the child's age, concepts and feelings associated with the body may be uncomfortable or unpleasant if the child has been sexually or physically abused. Therefore, the child may be hesitant to engage in this activity or may give a regressed, impoverished version to minimally comply with the task.

It is important for you to make a "mental note" of various aspects of the child's self-portrait, but this will be explored in further detail in later chapters. This first exercise of the self-portrait is to assess how the child sees himself or herself as the journey toward recovery is started.

Processing: If the child you are working with seems resistant or overwhelmed, extreme care must be used. You will need to be ready to respond with sensitivity and support for the child's feelings during this (or any of the activities in this book).

After the child has finished the drawing, ask him or her to tell you about it. Questions such as "How do you feel about this picture?" will allow the child to explore feelings he or she might have about himself or herself.

The following case example will illustrate how one sexually abused child processed this activity.

Case Example: *Donna*

Brief Case History: Donna was a 7-year-old sent to our facility from out of state. She lived with her father and stepmother and her 8-year-old stepsister. The father and stepmother had been married for a little more than 2 years at the time of referral.

Donna was referred to our program from a psychologist in a bordering state. The referral was made due to the complexity of this case. Donna previously had lived with her mother and stepfather, where she was exposed to alleged satanic, ritualistic, sexual abuse. Her father fought and won custody of his daughter when she was 4 years old. At that time, her father was alone and drinking quite heavily. Donna found herself taking care of her dad. She would clean the house and fix dinner. Donna spent every other weekend and all summer with her mother. It was during her summer visits that most of the alleged abuse occurred.

During her summer visits, Donna was exposed to her mother's religious cult activities. She described her mother and grandmother as "good witches" and told her psychologist that multiple perpetrators had sexually touched and penetrated her. She came to the attention of the referring psychologist due to Donna's sexual acting-out behavior. Donna revealed that she had been sexually touching numerous children who were friends of her father and stepmother. The psychologist decided that inpatient hospitalization was needed to assess this situation completely and to decide the best therapeutic course for this severely traumatized child.

Upon interview, Donna presented herself as an attractive, quite precocious, and verbally fluent 7-year-old. She had shoulder-length dark hair and beautiful brown eyes. Donna acted "parentified" and mature as she described her own sexual acting-out behavior. She described herself as a victim of abuse by numerous perpetrators as well as an "abuser." She also stated that she "abused herself."

Donna was interviewed with open-ended questions about the history of her molestation. She directed the conversation, explaining what she meant by "abuse." She stated that she was sexually molested and described her mother and maternal grandmother as fondling her vaginal area by stroking it. Donna actually demonstrated by moving her finger back and forth with gentle movements. She described this as arousing her. She also stated that they put various objects in her, such as various household objects, small sticks, and so on, as well as "sexual body parts." When asked to explain further, Donna said her uncles would put their penis in her vagina.

Donna explained that she did not tell for two reasons: (a) Sometimes she liked it and didn't want it to end, and (b) she was threatened never to tell the secret. At times she was physically forced to have sex—she was slapped if she said "no." Donna stated that she had actively "touched" other children sexually for several years, including her stepsister and the baby-sitter's children, friends, and children at school. She described herself as totally out of control when it came to acting out sexually.

Donna also described herself as actively dissociating during many of the sexual acts perpetrated on her. She described "going in the walls, into the light, and floating above herself." When asked to describe "floating above herself," Donna described her "spirit" as leaving her body and stated that she did this "as long as I didn't have to watch it happen." Her father and stepmother found it difficult to hear about all of the sexual acting-out behavior presented by Donna. They described her as otherwise a very obedient and well-behaved child. They were very worried about the stepsister and were rather fixated on their concern with Donna's chronic masturbating behavior.

Example of Activity #2

Donna was asked to draw a picture of herself as complete as possible (see Illustration 2.1). Donna and her therapist then talked about her drawing.

Therapist Well, Donna, tell me about your drawing.
Donna I drew myself with makeup on because I think it makes me look older, and I'm singing.
T How do you feel about looking older?
D Well, it just seems that I am older than 7, after all I've been through.
T You feel older than 7.
D Yeah.
T Would you like to feel more like 7?
D Yeah. I wish I could be more like my friends. (sad face)
T Well, that's what we'll be working on. Helping you to be more like a 7-year-old.

Clinical Impressions: The picture of Donna looked much older than her age. She appears with long, dark eyelashes and her cheeks look

Illustration 2.1.

like she has blush on them. This is typical of a child who has been made to behave like a grown woman in many respects. Her body language matched her drawing. She sat on the chair in a seductive manner, with legs spread open. At times she would cross her legs and sit in a pseudomature manner, flipping her hair back, and would talk as if she were much older.

The picture also reflected another aspect of her. She loved to sing and often sang in her therapy sessions. She really had a lovely voice and was proud of her talent in this area.

Donna's individual therapy addressed her traumatic experiences, and the milieu focused on allowing her to begin experiencing more age-appropriate play.

This is the example of an extremely open and pseudomature child. Many other abused children will not behave as openly as Donna. Some traumatized children are very leery of revealing anything about themselves. They may draw a very regressed drawing, capturing the notion that, emotionally, they are developmentally fixed at a younger age. Other children may refuse to do this activity, feeling completely inadequate.

It is important to instruct resistant children that they can draw stick figures if they choose. You may need to talk them through the activity, encouraging them to draw various aspects of themselves. Remember, this activity is to help build rapport. This should be presented as a fun activity and that there are no grades. Perhaps the child would be willing to draw something else that is less stressful. Allow this to occur and realize that this just lets you know where the child is in his or her recovery.

❏ Activity #3: My Family

Objective: To assist the child in seeing himself or herself in relation to the family.

This activity is designed to assess how the child views and fits into his or her family. Again you will be able to make an assessment regarding the child's emotional maturity via the picture and who he or she views as being a part of the family unit.

Kaufman and Wohl (1992) aptly state, "The family as an inter-active system is more powerful than the total individual members. The family is a dynamic force that influences the growth and devel-opment of the offspring. . . ." (p. 29). Through this process, the child's identification of the self emerges as a result of the internali-zation of the parental figures' feelings and values. Consequently, if positive feelings and values are present, the child most likely will develop a healthy, positive self-image. If negative values and feel-ings are consistently experienced, the child may develop an un-healthy, negative self-image.

A great deal of information regarding the child's perceptions of and involvement with the family may be reflected in this activity. The child may include additional people not normally included in the family, such as boyfriends, girlfriends, pets, extended family, and so on. Conversely, the child may elect to exclude people that normally would be included, such as himself or herself or other immediate family members.

The family drawing may elicit many different feelings as outlined previously. It is important not to pressure the child to include or exclude various people. It is possible that the child may choose not to draw his or her family at all. Remember that the purpose of this activity is to build rapport and gather information. Therefore, it is important not to pressure the child to complete the activity but, rather, use the resistance as an opportunity to explore the child's feelings.

Ages: Children ages 6 to 12 years should be able to complete this activity with little help. The younger or emotionally regressed child may provide little detail and may use stick figures.

Materials Needed: Activity sheet and pencils, crayons, markers, and/or colored pencils.

Instructions: Instruct the child to draw a picture of his or her family.

Note: Children no longer living with their biological family may need more assistance in terms of determining who they con-sider family. If the child asks who to include in the family drawing, a discussion of what family means to the child may be necessary. It is important not to suggest who the family should include.

Processing: After the child has drawn the picture of his or her family, it is helpful to ask about the people who were drawn. Make sure to have the child label who everyone is. We have also found it beneficial to ask how each person in the picture is feeling. This just gives you more insight into how the child views the family dynamics.

Children may include various pets in the family. The more detail included, the more you can learn about the family. Remember, this is a continuation of the rapport-building phase of recovery. As stated previously, do not pressure the child if he or she does not want to elaborate on the drawing.

We have found that children, in general, enjoy this activity. However, some children have found it a difficult task, especially if a child has been removed from his or her birth family.

The following case example will illustrate how one emotionally abused girl processed this activity.

Case Example: *Carrie*

Brief Case History: Carrie was a 7-year-old who was living with her mother and her mother's female partner. Carrie's parents had been divorced for several years. Carrie was having little contact with her biological father, who was described as an alcoholic.

Carrie was referred to partial hospital treatment due to severe out-of-control, oppositional, and defiant behaviors; aggression directed toward others that included both verbal and physical aggression; sexualized behaviors; and extremely poor social skills. She was referred to more intensive treatment in the Partial Hospital Program following 2 years in outpatient therapy.

Prior to the hospitalization, Carrie's diagnosis included Attention Deficit/Hyperactivity Disorder, Oppositional Defiant Disorder, and Tourette's Syndrome. Her problematic behaviors in her public school setting included frequently getting out of her seat, getting on the floor and "acting like a puppy," and pestering other children to the point of total classroom disruption. Her teacher also described her as extremely aggressive toward others, which included attempting to strangle her classmates on two separate occasions.

At home, her mother described her in much the same way as her teacher. Carrie frequently would assault her mother and her partner. She would break household items for no apparent reason and would throw temper tantrums lasting up to 3 hours. During these episodes Carrie would yell obscenities, typical of Tourette's Syndrome.

Prior to the divorce of Carrie's parents, she frequently witnessed severe domestic violence between her parents over a several-year period. Carrie's mother claimed that Carrie was never directly involved in these altercations. However, it was clear that she was emotionally traumatized by living in this environment.

At the time of her admission to the program, Carrie's current living environment had not changed significantly. Although Carrie's mother and her partner did not engage in physical disputes, they displayed a replication of her biological parents' turmoiled relationship. Carrie's mother was still in a very submissive position in her current relationship. The mother's partner was extremely domineering and emotionally abusive to both Carrie and her mother.

In addition to Carrie's aggressive acting-out behaviors, she also exhibited sexual behavior problems. She would masturbate in public, including in her classroom and at friends' houses. Carrie's sense of personal boundaries were nonexistent. Carrie's mother did not know exactly where the sexualized behaviors stemmed from but suspected that Carrie's father may have been sexually inappropriate with her. Carrie had lived with her father following her parents' separation for approximately 1 year.

Example of Activity #3

Carrie was asked to draw a picture of her family as complete as possible (see Illustration 2.2) at the beginning of the session.

Carrie Okay, can I draw them any way I want to?
Therapist Yep, any way at all.

Mom

Dad

Carrie

Illustration 2.2.

C   (While drawing the picture) This is me. I have long, pretty hair.
    (*Note:* The mother had just "chopped" off most of her hair.)
T   Yes, I can see that.
C   This is my mom. She's got spiked hair.
T   Uh huh . . . and is there anyone else in your family?
C   Can I draw my puppy?
T   Sure, if you think your puppy is a part of your family.
C   I think I'll just draw my dad. . . . I'm done, what do I do now?
T   Well, can you tell me a little bit about each person in your family.
    I'll write the words, if you want me to be your secretary.

C   Okay. This is my mom and she has spiked hair. Can I write her name?

T   Sure, if you want to. It's your picture.

Carrie proceeded to write each person's name above his or her picture and then scribbled out her own name.

C   This is my dad and he is nice sometimes.

After the therapist wrote what she dictated, Carrie wrote, "*and* he is mean."

T   So sometimes your dad is nice and sometimes he is mean. What do you mean by that?

C   Well, sometimes he gets really mad and starts yelling and stuff.

T   What do you mean by "and stuff"?

C   I don't really want to talk about it.

T   That's okay. Can you tell me a little bit about yourself?

C   (A long pause)

T   It can be anything at all.

C   I am sometimes good and sometimes bad. I get detention and sometimes I don't. (This was when she scribbled out her name.) I don't need to write my name because you already know me.

T   You're right, I do. Do you want to tell me any more about yourself?

C   Nope. I'm done.

T   Well, you really worked hard on your picture. It looks like sometimes you feel pretty good about yourself and sometimes you don't. Maybe we can work together so that you are feeling good about yourself most of the time.

Clinical Impressions: Carrie's drawing (see Illustration 2.2) reflects many of her current issues as well as her fantasy that her mom and dad might reunite. Her drawing is fairly immature.

Carrie's drawing is interesting in that she portrayed herself with long hair when her mother just cut it off, per the request of her mother's partner. This may reflect her current anxiety over this because Carrie really loved her long, light brown hair. She also drew her mother with longer hair in addition to the spikes, when her mother really had only spiked hair. This could indicate some identity confusion.

Also noteworthy in Carrie's picture is the positioning of herself in relation to her parents. She placed herself in front of them, in the middle. She put distance between herself and her mother while having the father touch her long hair with his hand. Interestingly, she drew appendages on her hands but drew mitten-type hands (no fingers) on her parents. There was a greater emphasis on drawing the heads of each person (disproportionately large and a different color than she used for the rest of the drawing).

Carrie excluded her mother's current partner, even though the mother put greater emphasis on her partner being part of the family unit than Carrie's father. While including her father, she added "*and he is mean.*" This could reflect the violence she observed or how her mother felt toward him.

Although Carrie drew herself as the prominent person in the picture, she proceeded to scribble out her name when describing herself. This may indicate her lowered self-esteem.

Carrie also demonstrated her need to control by frequently asking to include things such as her pet and then choosing not to when given permission. It is important to allow the child to feel in control. One way to do this is by giving the child permission to direct the activity, and another is to respect the child when told he or she doesn't want to discuss a particular aspect of the drawing.

This is an example of a child who was fairly cooperative in drawing her family. Her picture was somewhat immature, but that is not necessarily unusual for abused children, who may reveal regressed drawings. Other children may not be as cooperative and may refuse to draw certain family members. Again, it is important to allow the child to feel free to control his or her drawing. Remember, this is part of the rapport-building phase of recovery, and you do not want to alienate the child by "being the boss."

❑ **Activity #4: Family Activity**

Objective: To assess how the child's family interacts in a family activity.

This activity is designed to assess not only how children see themselves in the family but also how they view interactions between each family member.

Kaufman and Wohl (1992) describe important aspects of the kinetic family drawing (KFD) when working with abused children. They point out that the separation-individuation problem inherent in incestuous families may be reflected in the drawings of incest survivors. The incestuous family often is enmeshed with one another in unhealthy ways that make the normal process of becoming more independent very difficult. This may be reflected in the lack of boundaries between family members. This may be portrayed by compartmentalization.

This activity is not designed to assess the degree of damage or to determine whether abuse has occurred. This is included as part of the rapport-building process. Therefore, if you desire further information on this as an assessment technique, we recommend reviewing Kaufman and Wohl's (1992) book as well as Malchiodi's (1990) book on using art therapy with abused children.

Art therapy is a specialized form of therapy that requires an advanced degree. It may be useful to enlist the services of an art therapist if you desire a thorough interpretation of the child's artwork.

Ages: This activity is designed for children ages 6 to 12. The younger or emotionally regressed child may include little detail or may use stick figures. Again, you may need to discuss who is included in the family (biological family, foster family, etc.).

Materials Needed: Activity sheet and pencils, crayons, markers, and/or colored pencils.

Instructions: Instruct the child to draw his or her family doing something together.

Note: Be sure the child includes himself or herself in the drawing. It is important to see how the child sees the family interactions. It is a statement of how the child views the family interactions and perceives himself or herself in the family setting (Kaufman & Wohl, 1992).

Processing: After the child finishes the picture, engage the child in a conversation about what the family is doing. We have found it helpful to ask the child how old he or she is in the picture. Sometimes, if a child has been removed from the birth family due to abuse or death of a parent, the child will put himself or herself in the picture as a baby.

As stated in the previous activity, it is also helpful to ask about how each family member feels while doing the activity drawn in the child's picture.

❏ Activity #5: My Animal Family

Objective: To allow the child to express how he or she sees various members of the child's family by labeling them as different animals.

This activity is designed to help in the assessment of how the child sees various members of the family. Many times children seem less threatened by animals. Therefore, this activity allows the children to project how they view various members of their family as different types of animals.

You, as the therapist, can learn a great deal about the child's view in regard to possible violence, roles people play in the family, dominant or submissive positions, and how the child sees himself or herself in relation to the rest of the family. Caution should be taken regarding the child's wish-fulfilling projections rather than actually drawing a reality-based version of the family.

Ages: This activity is designed for children who are proficient enough in their drawing to depict animals. Children who are 8 or 9 years old should have little difficulty with this task.

A variation of this activity would be to ask the child what animal each family member reminds him or her of, without having the child draw the animals. This variation may be used with younger, less proficient children or children resistant to drawing activities.

Materials Needed: Activity sheet and crayons, colored pencils, and/or markers.

Instructions: Instruct the child to draw a picture of each family member as an animal. Be sure the child includes himself or herself. The figures do not have to be engaged in an activity. If the child is unable to draw pictures of animals, he or she may just verbalize this activity to you.

Processing: After the child has completed the drawing, we have found it informative to ask the child who each animal is in the family and how each one feels. You also need to ask which animal depicts the child. Further questions about how each animal acts in the family and how they all get along can be very informative about family interactions.

❏ **Activity #6: My Three Wishes**

Objective: To allow the child to explore his or her wishes in life.

This activity is designed to have abused children explore magical thinking in terms of how they would handle complete power over their life. This activity will help in the assessment of how fragile the child may be.

The healthier child with better ego strength will list three wishes that most likely include a sense of realistic hope for the future. If the child continues to struggle with an overwhelming sense of pain, the three wishes may be unrealistic or reflect his or her sense of help-lessness, with statements such as "I wish I could just die or go away forever."

Ages: This activity is designed for children ages 6 to 12. Children who have difficulty writing words will need you to act as secretary, allowing them to dictate.

Materials Needed: Activity sheet and pencils, crayons, colored pencils, and/or markers.

Instructions: Instruct the child to think for a moment about his or her three most important wishes. Then ask, "If you could have any three wishes in the world, what would they be?" Then instruct the child to write or draw the three wishes.

Note: If you have a "magic wand," you can use it in this activity.

Processing: After the child has revealed three wishes, we have found it very informative to ask which is the most important wish and how the child feels about each wish. It is also informative to ask if the child could change a wish, which one it would be.

The following case example will illustrate how one multiply-abused child processed this activity.

Case Example: *Timothy*

Brief Case History: Timothy was an 8-year-old who was in the foster care system and a ward of Child Protective Services. Timothy was placed in the acute unit of the hospital due to an escalation in his acting-out behaviors in his foster home and in his Partial Hospital Program. These behaviors included verbal and physical aggression toward others, with an attempt to hit and then stab a staff member with scissors. This placement followed a lengthy stay in a Partial Hospital Placement in another facility.

Timothy was the oldest child in a sibling group of four. He previously had been involved in the state protective system for approximately 6 months prior to his most recent involvement of almost 1 year. Timothy was originally placed in protective custody following allegations of sexual molestation by his biological father.

Timothy was returned to his mother's custody and once again removed several months later following physical abuse at the hands of his mother.

Timothy was then placed in a foster home that was dominated by a strict disciplinarian father. This foster father was rather demanding and made demeaning comments to Timothy such as "You idiot . . . something's wrong with your f___ing brain." He was then sent to the acute unit of the hospital, as stated earlier, due to this foster family not being able to handle him.

Example of Activity #6

At the beginning of the session, Timothy presented as being totally withdrawn, lying on the floor in a fetal position in the Time-Out Room. After several minutes of sitting on the floor and encouraging him to engage in the session, Timothy was placed on one of our laps. *Note:* This is not recommended unless you have been working with a child for a lengthy period of time and the child trusts you enough to get into his or her physical or personal space.

At that point, Timothy was willing to look at his therapists and engage in conversation. He was removed from the Time-Out Room and we all walked into his room, where we were able to begin the session.

Timothy I want to show you my dinosaur pictures.
Therapists Okay.
T Do you know how old these dinosaurs are?
Th We would like to hear all about how old they are, but first we need to talk to you about a few things. What got you in the Time-Out Room this morning?
T Things haven't been going so well this morning.
Th How have your visits with Mom gone?
T Sometimes they're good and sometimes they're bad.

At this point, Timothy went into how difficult his visits have been and reviewed some of the things his mother used to do to hurt him in the past. He also elaborated on how difficult it had become in his foster home. It was then decided to go into the "Three Wishes" activity, because Timothy began to escalate during the discussion.

Th Timothy, if you could have any three wishes, what would they be?

T What do you mean if I had three wishes?

Th If you had any three wishes in the whole world, what would you wish for?

T (1) I would wish to live in a house all by myself.

Th You would live all alone?

T Yep! and (2) I would want $100.00.

Th $100.00 sounds like a lot of money to you.

T Yeah . . . and (3) I would want all the dinosaur movies in the world. I would just stay home and watch dinosaur movies.

Timothy's three wishes were processed further with him by exploring how it seems that he has a hard time trusting others and wants to be by himself, as well as feeling safer by himself. We then pursued how difficult it is for him to deal with his feelings regarding adult caregivers because he has been hurt by his parents and foster parents.

Clinical Impressions: Timothy is a troubled young man. He has a hard time trusting anyone. This activity allowed Timothy to have a sense of control over his out-of-control world, because he was able to fantasize about any three wishes he could have.

His three wishes seem to indicate that he has problems living with others. This is accurate, because he tends to remove himself from his peers. His wish to live by himself indicates that he has a difficult time trusting others and may be suggestive of an attachment problem. It is a little curious that he wishes to be alone, because he does demand so much attention from the staff. However, because he chose to place himself in a stress-free environment, alone with his movies, he may not need the constant attention from others.

Timothy's second wish of $100.00 is fairly indicative of young children and their perceptions of the value of money. To a young child, $100.00 seems like a lot of money, especially in this boy's history. He comes from a family of lower socioeconomic status. The third wish for an unlimited supply of dinosaur movies relates to his need for power. The symbol of the dinosaur seems to represent power to this young boy. He tries to surround himself with dinosaurs via coloring dinosaur pictures, watching movies such as *Jurassic Park* (over and over to the point that he gives exact details of the movie), and having toy dinosaurs.

This activity was a very nonthreatening way to engage this child and to gain insight into just how fragile he is at this point in his recovery. He continues to need large, powerful animals to protect him and seems to need distance from others.

This particular example shows how easy it is to work an activity like this into a therapy session and give the therapist ideas of what will work best with the child in future therapy sessions. Obviously, in this child's therapy, it would be a good idea to use dinosaurs and a doll house in play therapy to help Timothy work through his traumas.

This is an example of a completely distrusting and difficult child. In other cases, it has been extremely easy to engage the child in this activity right from the beginning of a session. It is usually a fun and fantasy-filled activity for the child. Some children do resist even giving a wish if they are severely depressed. In those cases, it might help to just ask for one wish. Sometimes it is also helpful to add, "If you had a magic wand and could have anything you wished for, what would it be?"

❏ Activity #7: Pieces of Me

Objective: To encourage the child to express himself or herself in a fun and creative way by making a collage.

This activity is designed to allow children to express themselves in another modality. Making collages is a common activity for children to engage in. It is less threatening for many children because they can cut and paste materials that already are created. So many abused children have such low self-esteem that drawing can be intimidating for fear of being judged. It is interesting to see what the child chooses as a representation of himself or herself.

Ages: This activity is designed for children ages 6 to 12. However, if the child is developmentally delayed, the concept of this activity may not be understood by the child; thus the activity would not be appropriate.

For the younger child, ages 6 to 8, it may be more beneficial to work one-on-one to assist the child in cutting, pasting, organizing the pictures on the sheet of paper and to help him or her remain more focused. The older child should have little difficulty with this activity and may want to work independently.

Materials Needed: A variety of magazines and/or pictures that can be cut up, a large sheet of paper, glue, and scissors.

Instructions: Instruct the child to sit at a table and think about himself or herself. While looking through the materials, tell the child he or she may cut out any words, phrases, or pictures that remind the child of himself or herself. When finished, have the child arrange the pictures on the large sheet of paper and glue them down any way the child chooses.

Processing: After the child completes the collage, we have found it helpful to ask the child to tell you about the collage. It can be informative to have the child go over each object on the collage and to tell you about how each object or picture reminds the child of himself or herself. It is also useful to ask which one is liked the most and least and why.

❏ Activity #8: The Looking Glass

Objective: To enable the child to see himself or herself from a different perspective by viewing his or her reflection in a mirror.

This activity is designed to assess how children see themselves from a different perspective. This allows children to be a bit more objective because they are encouraged to focus on details observed in a mirror. Children are amused by reflections and can have fun with this activity. However, the severely damaged child may be resistant to this task because any self-oriented task is threatening to the self-image.

Ages: This activity is designed for children without developmental delays and who are approximately 9 to 12 years old. The child must also be able to transfer images that he or she sees onto paper. Typically, this activity is too abstract for younger children.

Materials Needed: Large or handheld mirror; activity sheet; crayons, pencils, markers, and/or colored pencils.

Instructions: Instruct the child to look in a mirror and to study his or her face for a minute or two. Then ask the child to draw a picture or write about the reflection in the mirror.

Processing: After the child completes the drawing, we have found it helpful to follow up with questions about what he or she sees when looking in the mirror, what feelings are seen in the picture, and how the picture of the child in the mirror differs from the image of himself or herself in the mind. It is also informative to ask how it felt drawing the image instead of just drawing a self-portrait from memory.

❏ **Activity #9: I Like Me Because . . .**

Objective: To allow the child to explore various things about himself or herself that the child likes.
    This activity is designed not only to begin helping children recognize and verbalize positive statements about themselves but also to assess the child's feelings of self-worth. Abused children tend to have a damaged view of self. Building self-esteem becomes an important therapy goal.

Ages: This activity is designed for children ages 6 to 12. The younger or academically delayed child may need assistance with writing and/or spelling. Regardless of their age, children with significantly low self-esteem may need a great deal of encouragement and prompting to complete this activity.

Materials Needed: Activity sheet and pencils, colored pencils, crayons, and/or markers.

Instructions: Instruct the child to write at least five things that he or she likes about himself or herself.

Note: If the child has difficulty naming attributes, encourage the child by pointing out several positive qualities you have observed.

Children with significantly low self-esteem may have a difficult time identifying five things they like about themselves. These children may identify things that are not really connected with themselves but, rather, are a part of their world, such as "I have a nice house, my dog is cute, I have a nice teacher," and so on. This is acceptable at this stage of the recovery process.

Processing: After the child completes this activity, we have found it very helpful to process each statement by asking the child about each positive attribute. It is informative to ask which positive attribute the child likes the most and why, as well as any feelings he or she had while completing this activity.

❏ Activity #10: My Goals

Objective: To encourage the child to begin learning about setting goals for himself or herself regarding what the child wants to accomplish in therapy.

This activity is designed to assist the child in beginning to share "therapeutic goals" in a nonthreatening manner. Most abused children have a difficult time organizing thoughts and feelings, let alone setting goals.

It is important for abused children to learn goal setting so movement can be made from victim to survivor. As a victim, the child has been placed in a vulnerable position of being powerless, learning a sense of helplessness. For the child to heal, there must be movement from a position of powerlessness to a position of healthy empowerment.

This activity will assist in creating movement toward a sense of empowerment by allowing the child to set goals in a nonthreatening way. This can be accomplished by first having the child begin to think about the things he or she would like to change about himself or herself. These can become the child's therapeutic goals.

Ages: This activity is designed for children ages 6 to 12 who are able to understand the concept of change. The child with writing difficulties may need to dictate his or her responses to you. The resistant child may need your assistance in processing nonthreatening goals at this stage in the therapy to complete this activity.

Materials Needed: Activity sheet and pencils, crayons, colored pencils, and/or markers.

Instructions: Instruct the child to think of the things he or she would like to change about himself or herself. Then have the child write five things he or she would like to change about himself or herself. It is hoped that these will become guides for therapeutic goals.

Note: It will be important to assist the child to stay focused on changes in the "self" rather than attempt to change "others" (e.g., "I would like my mother to be nicer and quit hitting me.").

Processing: After the child has completed this activity, we have found it important to follow up with various questions about what changes the child would like to have happen, which change is the most important, and how he or she can make these changes happen. It's also informative to check out the child's feelings about these changes and whether he or she feels it is possible.

3

Feelings

Feelings are the reactions that occur within individuals as they respond to the world and the stimuli outside themselves. Feelings or emotions can be affected by people's thoughts and by what they see, hear, touch, smell, and sometimes by what they taste.

Many times, children who have been abused learn to stuff their feelings or emotions. Suppressing the feelings becomes another unhealthy coping mechanism. Abused children may use this technique as a way to keep their secret, pretend nothing has happened, and protect or care for themselves when the adult(s) around them are not keeping them safe. All too often children who have been abused have their feelings and emotions invalidated by others, which is yet another way they learn to "stuff" their feelings.

These children need to learn that everyone has feelings, and it is healthy and normal to feel a variety of feelings. They also need to develop an understanding that it is acceptable to experience any feeling. Feelings need to be viewed as comfortable or uncomfortable versus good or bad. Finally, they need to understand that feelings and/or emotions can be triggered by different situations and that people respond in different ways.

The goal of this chapter is to aid children in identifying various feelings. These feelings may be associated directly with the abuse or with the lasting effects of their abusive experiences. In addition, the goal includes helping children to learn how to communicate their feelings so that they are more able to control their feelings instead of their feelings controlling them. The ability to communicate feelings and emotions is a vital piece of the abused child's recovery and an essential skill in becoming a survivor.

The activities in this chapter are designed to assist children in identifying, confronting, and expressing various feelings that may be associated with their abuse history. As children begin to get in touch with feelings in general, they may become overwhelmed with a flood of feelings that have been repressed. You, as the therapist, need to be prepared for children to react in unpredictable ways. This may include an escalation in problematic behaviors, which can be as severe as aggression directed toward others or self-abusive behaviors.

It is important to provide children with the structure necessary for them to feel safe. Again, this goes back to having firmly established a strong therapeutic alliance so that the child has a sense of security, which is necessary as the child begins to confront his or her feelings.

As provided in the last chapter, this chapter also includes a few case studies to assist you in further understanding how some of these activities have been used in actual therapy situations. We have given a brief case history, an example of dialogue between the therapist and child during the activity, and clinical impressions of the child's work.

It is important to engage in a thorough processing of children's thoughts and feelings as they move forward. At the end of several of the activities listed in this book, you will find a "Processing" section. As you found in the last chapter, the "Processing" section is general. You most likely will add your own ideas as you get to know the child.

Prior to working on the activities in this chapter, you may want to read the "Message to the Kids," found in the Activity Book, or give it to the child to read. This introduces the concept of feelings to the child.

❏ Activity #11: Feelings Chart

Objective: To assist the child in identifying happy, angry, sad, scared, confused, and proud feelings.

This activity is designed to assist the child in learning six basic feeling words and linking each of these feeling words with a facial expression. It is important to have the child build a firm foundation in identifying feelings and labeling these feelings. It is only after children are able to put words with their feelings that they will begin to explore, sift through, and create a frame of reference for their own abuse histories.

Ages: Children ages 6 to 12 should be able to complete this activity with very few problems. It may be helpful to review different expressions associated with feelings prior to completing the chart.

Materials Needed: Activity sheet and colored pencils, crayons, and/or markers.

Instructions: Instruct the child to look at the feelings chart on the activity sheet. Discuss each identified feeling word. Then ask the child to complete the blank chart provided by drawing a face for each feeling. While the child is drawing each face, make sure it matches the feeling word.

Processing: Once the child is finished, it is important to review the pictures. While reviewing the pictures, you may want to ask additional questions, such as "Have you ever felt happy, sad, frustrated, scared, angry, or proud?" "Tell me about the times when you had these feelings." "Are there any feelings among these that you think you should not have?" Another idea is to have the child show each feeling with his or her own face.

❏ **Activity #12: How Would You Feel?**

Objective: To be able to express feelings associated with given life experiences depicted in various vignettes.

This activity is designed to assist children in moving from simply labeling feelings to matching their own feelings with the given life experiences depicted in the vignettes. This activity may begin to increase the child's anxiety level because inner feelings are elicited. It is important to help the child to begin differentiating between comfortable and uncomfortable feelings.

Ages: Children ages 6 to 12 should be able to complete this activity as long as they can read, or the vignettes need to be read to them. The given situations are on a rather concrete, simple level.

Materials Needed: Activity sheet and pencils, crayons, colored pencils, and/or markers.

Instructions: Instruct the child to read each vignette (this can be done alone or with your help). After reading the vignette, tell the child to write about his or her feelings associated with the given situation.

Processing: After the child has completed the activity, we have found it helpful to go over each vignette and ask the child various questions, such as "How would you feel in this situation?" "Tell me about a similar experience you had." "Which situation makes you feel most comfortable?" "Which situation makes you feel most uncomfortable?" You may find it more useful to process each vignette, as you will find in the following example.

The following case example will illustrate how one abused child processed this activity.

Case Example: *Amy*

Brief Case History: Amy was an 11-year-old who was in the Child Residential Treatment Center in the facility. She had been living in a shelter for 2 weeks prior to her hospitalization in our acute program and eventual placement in the Child Residential Program.

Amy had been taken away from her mother due to neglect as well as physical and sexual abuse by her mother's numerous boyfriends. Amy's biological mother had a history of prostitution and drug abuse.

During one visit, prior to being removed permanently, Amy was kidnapped by her mother and taken out of state. Several months later, she was located and Amy eventually was returned to the foster care system. This was really difficult for Amy. Her mother changed her name and dyed her hair another color. This reinforced her prior need to keep secrets.

Amy had been tried in two foster care placements. In the first one, she was sexually and physically abused by the foster family. She ran away from this home and was picked up by the police and placed back there due to the belief that she was not telling the truth. It was later found out that they had abused numerous children in their care, and they are now serving prison terms for that abuse.

The second placement was in a foster-adopt home. The foster mother was a professional single woman. This placement did not work out. Amy needed to be nurtured, and the foster mother was not a very warm and nurturing woman. She seemed to have excellent credentials, but it appeared doomed to fail due to the extreme differences in these two people.

After this failed, Amy was placed in a Time-Out Shelter, where she began running away and not complying with rules. Eventually she was hospitalized due to depression and oppositional behavior.

Example of Activity #12

Amy was asked to complete the vignettes. We then processed her work.

Therapist Tell me about what you wrote for the first situation on your activity sheet.

Amy I said that Sally was feeling excited and that is how I would feel.

T Tell me more about that.

A It means they are trying to be a friend and have a healthy relationship.

T   Tell me about your second one.

A   I would feel left out.

T   Tell me more about how you would feel left out.

A   I would feel pretty upset and maybe nervous, like I would be saying to myself, "What's going on?" and I'd probably shake inside.

T   What about the third situation about Brian?

A   I wrote down that I would feel scared.

T   What kinds of things would you be scared of?

A   Could be the wind or my mom being hurt or someone breaking in. . . . Lots of things could be happening.

T   It sounds like you felt that way with your mom when you were living with her.

A   Yeah. I felt that way a lot. (face looks sad)

T   It looks like that brings up a lot of scary feelings for you.

A   I think about my mom a lot. I wish I could see her again.

T   I bet you do.

A   On the last one, I said I would feel disrespected if treated that way. My boundaries would have been violated.

T   Tell me about what you mean by that.

A   Some people out there think that having boundaries is crazy. They don't know what it means. I have learned all about boundaries and keeping myself safe in this program.

T   Great work, Amy!

The rest of the session focused on Amy's feelings regarding her mother and the fact that she was missing her.

Clinical Impressions: It is clear from the answers that Amy gave that she still struggles with her feelings of abandonment and anxiety. She appears to be almost waiting for the other shoe to drop. She clearly doesn't trust her environment. She is still quite afraid and seems to feel powerless over things that have happened and are happening in her life.

She seems to be learning how to express her feelings in rather sophisticated terms (e.g., boundaries being violated), but she is still really in the beginning phase of recovery. She needs to develop a strong therapeutic bond with a long-term therapist to allow her to begin trusting others again, because she lost her therapist of 2 years when she switched programs. Amy also needs to develop coping strategies to keep herself safe. She is still very fearful.

Amy did very well with this activity. She enjoyed the one-on-one time. The vignettes allowed her to keep some emotional distance while still allowing her to process some of her own issues and feelings.

❑ **Activity #13: My Feelings**

Objective: To learn how to create and use "I feel" statements.

This activity is designed to assist the child in developing a healthy way to express feelings so that others are able to listen and understand. While working on this activity, the child is encouraged to use "feeling" words. It is important to note a frequent error made when making "I feel" statements. Thoughts are often substituted for feelings (i.e., "I feel good" or "I feel like I'm a volcano ready to explode"). Instead, the child needs to be stating, "I feel happy" or "I feel very angry."

Ages: Children ages 6 to 12 should be able to complete this activity as long as they can read and write. For those with reading or writing difficulties, the statements can be read by you aloud and the child can dictate the response.

Materials Needed: Activity sheet and pencils.

Instructions: Instruct the child to complete the "I feel" statements. As stated above, you may need to read the statements to the child and have the child dictate the response to you.

Processing: After the child has completed the vignettes, it is helpful to process the activity with him or her by asking additional questions, such as "Tell me about the different feelings you stated in your 'I feel' statements. Which 'I feel' statement was the most comfortable for you to make? Why?" "Which 'I feel' statement was the most uncomfortable for you to make? Why?"

The following case example will illustrate how one abused child processed this activity.

Case Example: *Samantha*

Brief Case History: Samantha was a 7-year-old who was referred by her mother following a domestic violence episode between the mother and father. She was seen in a private practice setting for therapy related to the traumatic effects of witnessing a rather severe domestic violence episode.

Samantha is the oldest of two children born to parents who have been married for approximately 10 years. She has a younger sister, age 4. This was a planned pregnancy. Both parents work in business establishments.

Her mother called for the appointment after Samantha had experienced bad dreams associated with the fight. According to Samantha, her father came home drunk and her parents argued over something. Then, her father got angry and started choking her mother. He pushed her into a table and there were marks on her mother's neck. Mother also had red eyes and a hurt shoulder and back. Samantha called out for the neighbors. Someone called 911 and the father was arrested.

Before the police arrived, the mother took Samantha and her sister to the neighbor's house. As Samantha related the incident, it was clear that this was a very frightening experience for her. She stated that her father had a drinking problem. This seemed to consume Samantha. She feared that anyone who drank alcohol would get angry and hurt someone else.

At the time of referral, Samantha was experiencing several post-traumatic effects, such as intense fear, agitated behavior, scary dreams, flashbacks, difficulty falling asleep, hypervigilance, and startle response.

On the first visit to the office, Samantha cried as she related the incident. She stated that she had been having terrible dreams about the incident. She missed her father, who was staying with relatives, and seemed to feel guilty for yelling out for the neighbors.

On the next visit, she stated she was still having bad dreams in which her hands and feet were small. She felt scared. She couldn't get back to sleep. She was happy her father was back in the home, and he stated that he promised not to drink anymore. She was happy that her parents were going for therapy to work on their problems.

Samantha's mother related that she and her husband decided to seek therapy before the situation got any worse. She now realized just how traumatized her daughter was as a result of their fights. She also realized that she was not responsible for her husband's behavior and felt that because he was willing to seek help, she would give it a chance. She stated that if he continued to drink, she would seek a divorce.

The parents have since participated regularly in therapy, and the father did go to court on the domestic violence charge. He has complied and is doing well in therapy. This is unusual in that he is taking responsibility for his behavior and sees that it is a repeat of his father's behavior. He does not want to be like his father, according to their marital therapist. He has not been drinking since the fight.

Therapy with Samantha consisted of play therapy, artwork, and games. Samantha seemed to relate very well to these mediums. She was fairly verbal and would talk during the play. There was lots of evidence of hypervigilant behavior during the sessions. She was easily startled, and her eyes darted all over the room as she attempted to remain involved in play.

During one of her sessions, while still in the earlier phases of treatment, Samantha was asked to complete Activity #13 to assess how she was processing feelings in a general way.

Example of Activity #13

Samantha was given Activity #13 and asked to complete the sentences and then they were discussed.

Therapist Samantha, I want you to complete these sentences with your feelings.
Samantha Oh, I can do that.
T Tell me what you wrote for your first sentence.
S I said, "I feel happy when I watch TV!"

T It sounds like you really like to watch TV.

S I have my own television in my room. I watch it sometimes when I can't get to sleep. Mom lets me.

T You do? What is your problem about sleeping?

S I get scared at night and I don't want to go to sleep. I used to sleep with Mom and Dad when I was scared.

T I know. We've talked about that, haven't we?

S Yeah. I can't sleep there anymore. . . .

T You don't look too happy about that.

S I just get so scared at night. I worry that someone is going to break in the house. I get scared if Mom and Dad aren't still in the living room when I go to bed.

T I know. We've talked about that. Having the television on seems to help you get to sleep.

S I fall right asleep.

T What do you have for your next sentence?

S "I feel sad when I have to go to bed sometimes, or when my parents argue."

T Nighttime seems scary for you. Do you still worry about your parents arguing?

S I still worry that they will fight again. My dad hasn't been drinking and they don't argue anymore, but I am worried that he won't keep his promise. Can cigarettes make you drunk?

T No, cigarettes can't make you drunk. You still seem very worried.

S Yeah, but not as much.

T Good. How about your next sentence—what did you write? (While completing this sentence, Samantha did ask what *frustrated* meant and was given an example.)

S "I feel frustrated when I can't find my shoes."

T Does that happen very often?

S Sometimes I forget to leave them in my room and my mom has to help me find them.

T What did you write down about scared feelings?

S "I feel scared when the bathroom light's not on or the hall light."

T It sure does sound like it is still so difficult for you at night. Does it help to have the bathroom light or the hall light on?

S Yeah. Mom just sometimes forgets and turns it off. Then I remind her that I need it on.

T   Does she turn it back on?

S   Yes, but sometimes I'm still scared.

T   We'll have to do a lot of work on that, won't we?

S   Yeah.

T   Okay. What did you write down for the next sentence?

S   "I feel angry when. . . ." I don't really get angry. Maybe when I get in trouble sometimes.

T   You don't feel angry very much?

S   No.

T   Do angry feelings bother you?

S   Yes. When my father gets angry or when my mother gets really angry at my father, I'm worried they will fight again.

T   Sometimes people argue but don't hit each other.

S   I know. My aunt and uncle argue, but they don't fight.

T   So fighting to you is hurting each other?

S   Yeah. I think it happens when people drink alcohol.

T   Sometimes people drink alcohol and don't get drunk. Did you know that?

S   Yeah, but my dad gets drunk.

T   What did you write down for the last sentence?

S   "I feel proud when like if I get my spelling test right."

T   I bet you do feel proud when you do well in spelling.

The session ended shortly after the discussion.

Clinical Impressions: Clearly, Samantha is still very troubled by the domestic violence. She is still having trouble sleeping, although she is not having bad dreams any longer. She has been having difficulty staying in her room and her parents are frustrated with her (and her sister, who is having similar sleep problems).

It is important to note that although leaving the television on at night would not be recommended for all children, in this case, the television is soothing to this child and provides background noise. She does not use it to manipulate her parents.

In a strict behavioral method, leaving the television on probably would not be recommended. But we feel it is important to listen to what children are saying about their internal struggles. This child was very clear about how this helped to ease her anxiety. Children are sometimes our best teachers of what they are feeling. We need to respect that and at the same time help them to work through their conflicts.

The sentences gave Samantha an opportunity to process many of her feelings. She was able to branch into discussions about fears and worries she still has. At this time, keeping her focused is not too difficult as long as she is engaged in an activity. Although she is sitting, she is in perpetual motion.

At some point it also may be necessary to assess Samantha for Attention Deficit Disorder (ADD). Her last teacher did question this, but due to the domestic violence situation, it was hard to assess whether she was hypervigilant due to the domestic violence or whether she was also distractible due to ADD.

It has been only 4 months since the first session. This will need to be assessed as she begins to resolve the trauma from the domestic violence. The teacher will need to provide additional information as the year progresses. Samantha will need to be assessed as to her ability to attend school and whether there has been a change since the parents have begun therapy.

Samantha is a clear picture of just how much children are affected by their parents' domestic violence. Neither she nor her sister are given corporal punishment, yet Samantha is an extremely fearful child. Both she and her sister struggle with generalized anxiety reactions. They are both very sensitive and seem to cry easily. Even with the best possible scenario for this situation (e.g., parents are doing really well in therapy and they have been using new communication techniques), Samantha is still a long way from resolving this trauma.

❏ **Activity #14: Feelings Pictures**

Objective: To explore how to associate feelings with life experiences.

This activity is designed to assist children in directly connecting their life experiences with various feelings and practicing how to communicate feelings. The child will be asked to relate various experiences associated with six different feelings.

Ages: Children ages 6 to 12 should be able to complete this activity as long as they can draw at least stick figures.

Materials Needed: Activity sheets and pencils, crayons, colored pencils, and/or markers.

Instructions: Instruct the child to draw pictures of a time when he or she felt happy, sad, scared, angry, frustrated, and proud.

Note: The younger or developmentally delayed child may find it easier to relate experiences verbally rather than draw pictures. In that case, write what the child tells you on the pages provided.

Processing: After the child has completed each picture, it is important to process the picture with him or her. Questions we have found helpful include the following: "Tell me about your picture(s)." "How come you were feeling happy, sad, scared, angry, frustrated, proud?" "Which picture was the most comfortable to draw? Why?" "Which picture is the most comfortable to talk about? Why?" "Which picture was the most uncomfortable to draw? Why?" "Which picture is the most uncomfortable to talk about? Why?"

❏ **Activity #15: Flying With Feelings**

Objective: To continue the process of identifying feelings by using the medium of art and colors.

This activity is designed to assist the child in exploring feelings through a different medium—color. This is a fun, nonthreatening activity that helps to break any tension that may be building from the previous activities. It also may provide some information for you regarding how the child uses various colors to express feelings.

Ages: Children ages 6 to 12 should be able to complete this activity as long as they can relate the concept of color to a feeling.

Materials Needed: Activity sheet and crayons, colored pencils, and/or markers.

Instructions: Instruct the child to color the hot-air balloon. Make sure the child is aware that each part of the balloon represents a different feeling and encourage the child to carefully choose colors he or she associates with that feeling.

Note: This activity may take some discussion with the younger or developmentally delayed child. It is important to tell the child that there is no "right" or "wrong" color associated with a particular feeling.

Processing: After the child has completed the balloon, it is important to process the drawing with the child by asking, "Tell me about your balloon." "Which color do you like the most? Why?" "Which color is not your favorite? Why?"

❏ **Activity #16: Feelings Collage**

Objective: To explore feelings by means of picking pictures associated with feelings.
    This activity is designed to encourage children to express their feelings in a relatively nonthreatening manner. It is interesting to see what children choose as representations of their feelings when looking through magazines, pictures, and so on.

Ages: Children ages 6 to 12 should be able to complete this activity with some assistance.

Materials Needed: A variety of magazines and/or pictures that can be cut up, a large sheet of paper, glue, and scissors.

Instructions: Instruct the child to sit at a table and think about his or her feelings as the child looks through the magazines and/or pictures. Tell the child he or she may cut out any words, phrases, or pictures. Encourage the child to keep cutting until he or she feels finished. Have the child arrange the pictures on the large sheet of paper and glue them down any way he or she chooses.

Note: The younger or developmentally delayed child may need more assistance regarding choosing various pictures, words, and so on that reflect the child's feelings.

Processing: After the child has completed the collage, it is important to process the collage with him or her by asking, "Tell me about your collage." "Tell me about the different feelings expressed in your collage." "Why do you feel that way?" "Tell me more about your collage."

❑ **Activity #17: Feelings Puppets**

Objective: To learn how to express feelings using puppets.

This activity is designed to help the child practice identifying and expressing feelings in a fun and nonthreatening way. Children tend to express their feelings freely when using the medium of puppet play.

Ages: Children ages 6 to 12 will enjoy this activity.

Materials Needed: Lunch-size paper bags; crayons, markers, colored pencils, and/or paint.

Instructions: Instruct the child to sit at a table, take at least three paper bags, and choose three feelings he or she would like to draw on the puppets. Have the child draw the face on the folded side of the bag, reflecting how the puppet feels.

You may expand this project by having the child act out plays, various feelings, or make up stories using the puppets.

Note: The younger or developmentally delayed child will need more assistance in reviewing facial expressions reflective of various feelings.

Processing: After the child has completed the puppets, it is important to process the activity by asking, "Tell me about your puppets and how each one feels." "Which one do you like the most? Why?" "Which one do you like the least? Why?" "How can your puppets help you express feelings?"

❑ **Activity #18: Feelings Mask**

Objective: To explore what is felt on the inside and how this is portrayed to others.

This activity is designed to encourage children to explore their inner feelings and how that is manifested on the "outside." The child may find that the feelings expressed outwardly are much different than what is felt on the "inside." This activity may be very difficult for some children, who may need a great deal of encouragement and/or processing before they are able to differentiate between the inner feelings and the outward expression of those feelings.

Ages: Children ages 6 to 12 will find this a fun activity.

Materials Needed: Two paper plates; stapler or glue; Popsicle sticks or tongue depressors; and crayons, markers, colored pencils, and/or paints.

Instructions: Instruct the child to sit at a table and take two paper plates. Ask the child to think how he or she feels most of the time on the inside and to draw that feeling on one of the paper plates.

Next, ask the child how others see him or her on the outside and draw that expression on the other paper plate. Then instruct the child to either staple the back of the plates together or glue them together. Be sure to place the stick between the plates prior to securing them together.

Note: The concept of "outer" and "inner" feelings may be a difficult concept for the younger or developmentally challenged child. Therefore, those children will need a lot of assistance with this concept. If the concept is too difficult, the child may just draw how he or she feels and make it into a mask.

Processing: After the child has completed the mask, it is important to process the activity by asking, "Tell me about the feelings you have drawn on your plates." "Which one is how you feel on the inside? Why?" "Which one is how other people see you? Why?" "What makes it difficult to show your inside feelings to others (if the two feelings are different)?"

❏ **Activity #19: Scrapbook of Feelings**

Objective: To learn how to collect various items that reflect feelings of various life experiences and to organize them in a scrapbook.

This activity is designed to teach children how to organize important feelings they may have felt in regard to different experiences shared over time. This book can be organized in the form of separate feelings sections, chronologically or by events. This activity is designed to take place over a period of time. It may be an ongoing activity that is done in addition to other activities.

Ages: Children ages 6 to 12 years should be able to begin this project with assistance.

Materials Needed: Buy a scrapbook or make your own. Have available magazines, other pictures, glue, crayons, markers, colored pencils, and scissors. The child may choose to bring in various items that represent various feelings they have experienced to be included in the scrapbook.

Instructions: Instruct the child to begin collecting various items, magazine pictures, phrases, photographs, and so on that have meaning to the child and/or represent feelings that have been experienced. Help the child decide how to organize the scrapbook (i.e., by feelings, time frames, or events). Then instruct the child to begin putting the items on paper in the scrapbook. The child needs to know that this is a project that may take some time to complete. Allow the child to be as creative as he or she desires.

Note: The older child will be able to be more independent and may enjoy this activity more than the younger or developmentally delayed child. The older child may even want to take the scrapbook home and work on his or her own, but the younger child may do best leaving the scrapbook with you.

Processing: After the child has completed the scrapbook, a session should be set aside to go through the entire scrapbook, and the items should be processed. It may be helpful to ask, "Tell me about the items you have collected." "Tell me about the feelings each one represents. Why?"

4

Boundaries

Boundaries can be defined as limits or borders that can be experienced as either physical, emotional, or sexual. Children who have been abused have experienced a violation of their boundaries. Their sense of personal control in their world was taken away. They were left feeling powerless over their ability to protect their personal space. Often, these children have not learned the right to privacy or the right to emotional distance and separateness due to their abusive experiences.

When children are beaten or sexually molested, it is fairly clear that their boundaries have been violated. It is the less visible abuse, such as emotional or psychological abuse, that is often ignored. Children who have been verbally assaulted, rejected, isolated, or undernurtured also have had their boundaries violated. For all of these children boundary issues are significant.

Abused children's sense of boundaries or limits becomes diffuse. They are uncertain and confused regarding the appropriateness of others' behavior toward them as well as their behavior toward others. Many times, these children become "reactive" abusers by violating other people's personal space. This is sometimes a result

57

of the diffuse boundaries, but other times it is a way to regain their sense of power and control lost in the original abuse. This can be exhibited either physically or emotionally.

In most families of abuse-reactive children, the parents have not provided a model of good boundary management for family members (Gil & Johnson, 1993). Appropriate boundary development is essential for abuse-reactive and abused children. Often, these children have been exposed to either no boundaries or "loose" boundaries in their home setting. This could include the parent(s) and child bathing together, sleeping together on a regular basis, inappropriate kissing (tongue kissing), questionable attire (often walking around with very little on), and/or sharing inappropriate sexual materials (videos, pictures, magazines, stories).

As a therapist, it is important to assess your own personal approach to maintaining appropriate boundaries. Although some therapists feel very comfortable hugging young children, this can be misinterpreted by the child. However, nurturing children is an important part of the therapeutic process.

Briere (1992) aptly points out that the abuse survivor's dependence on the therapist is a healthy process. He suggests that this might be reframed as attachment rather than dependency. The client needs to be nurtured so that his or her therapy-appropriate needs can be met. In addition, the client must be encouraged toward the process of individuation. This process includes communicating appropriate boundaries and providing support and validation.

In order to provide appropriate boundaries while still nurturing the child, the therapist may want to limit frontal hugging and switch to hugging from the side. This may be less stimulating to sexualized children and less threatening to physically abused children. Some therapists prefer to shake hands with the extremely sexualized child who seeks constant body contact.

The goal of this chapter is to assist the child in understanding the importance of healthy boundaries as well as ways to establish them. The development of healthy boundaries is another important step in the child's recovery process.

The activities in this chapter are designed to assist children in identifying, differentiating, and developing boundaries in their environment. Because abused children's boundaries have been violated, the activities in this chapter may be very difficult for some children to complete without experiencing a great deal of pain and anxiety.

Some children may become altogether resistant when addressing the issue of boundaries. Patience, persistence, and understanding will be especially important at this stage in the child's recovery.

A couple of case studies are included in this chapter to assist you in further understanding how some of these activities have been used in actual therapy situations. As we have done in the preceding chapters, we have given a brief case history, an example of dialogue between the therapist and child during the activity, and clinical impressions. We hope this helps you in your own work with abused children.

Several of the activities in this chapter may elicit feelings related to past maltreatment. This is a normal aspect of trauma recovery work. The story provided in this chapter seems to provoke a lot of discussion in group therapy. This is a time when some children begin to self-disclose. They may relate to various aspects of the story and share their own experiences.

Although this chapter is still focused on the beginning stages of trauma recovery, some children may trust enough to jump ahead. It is important to stay focused on the activity while allowing the child to relate feelings that stem from prior (or current) maltreatment.

The Activity Book includes a "Message to the Kids." You may want to read this to the child or give it to him or her to read. This is a general introduction to the concept of "boundaries." This can then be placed in the child's folder, along with the other "Messages."

❑ **Activity #20: Boundaries—Dot to Dot**

Objective: To learn the concept of "boundaries."

This activity is designed to assist the child in beginning to understand what boundaries are in a very concrete yet fun manner. Many times, children who have experienced abusive interactions with others lose their sense of boundaries. Children who have not been abused seem to have a natural instinct regarding personal space. This instinct serves to protect the child.

When this natural instinct is lost, the child is left vulnerable to violations by others. It also tends to render some children vulnerable to violating the boundaries of others. The sense of boundaries is a vital skill for abused children to learn in the healing process.

Ages: This activity is designed for children ages 6 to 12.

Materials Needed: Activity sheet and pencil, crayons, markers, or colored pencils.

Instructions: Instruct the child to connect the dots and color in the picture provided. While the child is connecting the dots, discuss the physical boundary created by the connected lines and the idea that everyone has physical boundaries that should not be violated.

Note: The older child may think this is too simple; however, he or she needs to be encouraged to complete the activity and participate in a discussion of boundaries. This activity is not appropriate for developmentally delayed children who have not yet mastered the concept of connecting dots.

Processing: After the child has completed the activity, it is helpful to process with questions such as "What do you think boundaries are?" "Does everyone have their own boundaries? Why?" "How do you think people violate physical boundaries? Why?" "Has anyone ever violated your physical boundaries? How?"

❏ Activity #21: Personal Space

Objective: To gain an understanding of *personal space.*

This activity is designed to assist the child in developing an understanding and sense of personal space. As stated earlier, abused children typically have lost the concept of personal space—what personal space is and how to protect their own personal space.

This activity is only a starting point for the child in developing skills to protect his or her personal space and learning to respect others' personal space. As you continue to work with the child, this activity will provide you with a concrete reference point that may be used with the child from time to time.

Ages: Children ages 6 to 12 should be able to complete this activity with some assistance.

Materials Needed: Activity sheet and crayons, markers, and/or colored pencils.

Instructions: Instruct the child to color in the personal space noted on the activity sheet. As the child is working on coloring in the personal space, discuss what this space means to each person. Children will typically ask to color in the rest of the picture. This is fine as long as you are certain that they have a clear understanding of the personal space concept.

Note: As long as the concept of personal space is understood, there should be very little difficulty with this activity. In fact, younger children have a lot of fun with this activity.

Processing: After the child has completed the activity, it is important to process the activity to verify that he or she understands this concept. We have found it helpful to ask, "Tell me about your personal space—what is it?" "How do people violate personal space?" "What happens when people violate someone's personal space?" "How has your personal space been violated?"

❏ **Activity #22: This Is Me!**

Objective: To develop further understanding of the concepts of physical boundaries and personal space.

This activity is designed to assist the child in developing further understanding regarding the concept of physical boundaries and personal space. This activity will help the child move from the external notion of what boundaries are to a concrete application of this principle by having the child actually participate in the process of making a life-size portrait. The child lies down and allows the therapist to trace his or her body.

Ages: This is usually a fun experience for children of all ages; however, some children may be apprehensive and resistant to having their body traced by someone else.

Materials Needed: A large sheet of butcher paper, pencil, crayons, markers, paint, and scissors.

Instructions: Instruct the child to lie down on his or her back on the butcher paper. Trace an outline of the child's body with a pencil. Then instruct the child to cut along the lines. He or she then can color in the body as desired. As the child is cutting out his or her figure and coloring, discuss the concepts of physical boundaries and personal space. It is important to help the child link up the reality of his or her own physical boundaries and personal space with the figure being cut out and colored.

This activity may raise a lot of issues of previous violations. This may result in some inappropriate "acting-out" by the child, especially the child with limited verbal communication skills. The therapist should be prepared to deal with any problematic behaviors and process any fears, apprehensions, or anger felt by the child.

Note: Children should not be forced to do this (or any other) activity if they are uncomfortable with it. Instead, a discussion of the child's feelings is in order.

Processing: After the child has completed this activity, it is important to process how it felt to do this type of activity. It can be helpful to ask, "How did it feel to have someone trace your body?" "What did you learn about your own physical boundaries and personal space?" "Tell me about your body portrait."

❑ Activity #23: My Personal Space

Objective: To reinforce the notion of a healthy sense of personal space.

This activity is designed to reinforce the notion of a personal space around the child's body. Again, it is important for children who have been abused to develop an understanding and a sense of a healthy personal space. Children need to gain a healthy perspective regarding not being too rigid yet not allowing others to disrespect their boundaries.

This is a difficult concept for children, because developmentally they may not understand the limits of healthy and unhealthy interactions with others. However, when older children or adults do not respect the child's personal space, it leaves the child in the position of setting and maintaining appropriate and safe boundaries. This responsibility places the child in a vulnerable position. This activity is designed to help the child with this arduous task.

Ages: This activity is designed for children ages 6 to 12 as long as the child is able to draw a figure (a stick figure is acceptable).

Materials Needed: A piece of paper; pencils, crayons, markers, and/or colored pencils.

Instructions: Instruct the child to draw a picture of himself or herself and then to color in the area that the child believes is his or her personal space. It will be interesting to note how much personal space the child colors around the body.

Note: This activity can serve as another yardstick of the child's comfort level, which may indicate a need for further work in this area. For example, if the child has a very small personal space, it may indicate a lack of protection for the child, or an unreasonably large area may indicate the child's need for protection. Either way, the following process questions may help you assess where the child is with this concept.

Processing: After completing this activity, it is important to process the child's feelings regarding personal space. We have found it helpful to ask, "Tell me about your personal space on your picture." "Is this the same as the other picture you colored in or is it different? Why?" "Is your personal space the same with everyone you know, or do you have a different space for different people? Why or why not?"

The following case example will illustrate how one abused child processed this activity.

Case Example: *Freddy*

Brief Case History: Freddy was a 10-year-old admitted to the residential treatment facility due to his violent aggression toward others, rage attacks, and sexualized behaviors. Freddy's out-of-control behaviors, which had been ongoing for years, seemed to be getting worse as he got older. He had been involved in very little outpatient or other kinds of therapy because he lived in a rural area and few services were available.

Prior to Freddy's placement in the Residential Treatment Center (RTC), he was living in a group home. This placement came after multiple placements in foster homes beginning at age 4. Freddy was removed from his parents' care after there had been numerous reports made regarding physical abuse and neglect. From the time that he was placed in foster care, he was known as being a "difficult" child.

Relatively little was known about Freddy's first 4 years of life because of his sketchy records. The records indicated that he was an only child. His mother apparently stayed at home and his father was an automobile mechanic. Freddy's father would frequently drink before coming home and then would become very violent to both Freddy and his mother. During the day his mother apparently would isolate herself, allowing Freddy to fend for himself.

Eventually, Freddy was taken into custody by the state following several reports of neglect and physical and emotional abuse. Shortly following his placement, Freddy began to exhibit behaviors consistent with sexual abuse. He frequently masturbated in his day care placement and in his foster home. He invaded others' personal space by hugging, attempting to touch others in their private areas, kissing other children and adults; re-created sexual behaviors in play with dolls and stuffed animals; and used a great deal of "potty" language.

Freddy's behaviors continued and worsened over the years. He began getting kicked out of foster home after foster home because his foster parents could not deal with Freddy's out-of-control behaviors. In addition, his sexual behaviors were getting more and more assaultive over the years. Freddy began to perpetrate sexual acts against younger children and was sexually abusive to animals.

The following example was taken from a session approximately 3 months into Freddy's placement in the RTC program. Therapy was extremely difficult with Freddy because he seemed to easily get on emotional "overload" and become very violent. When he was not acting out aggressively, he would frequently run up to adults and give hugs without getting prior permission.

When the adult would give a clear message regarding the need to respect personal space, Freddy would feel rejected and then escalate his behaviors.

Example of Activity #23

Prior to asking Freddy to draw his personal space, a discussion was held regarding personal space. This included what personal space means and that each person's personal space may be different.

Therapist Now I want you to draw a picture of yourself and color in the area around yourself that shows your personal space.

Freddy But I don't like to draw pictures of myself.

T Freddy, however you draw a picture of yourself is okay. I'm not a very good artist myself, look (drew a stick figure.) See, this is the best drawing I can do of myself. Why don't you give it a try.

F I can draw better than that. Can I use any colors I want to?

T   Sure you can, it's your picture.

F   There . . . this is a picture of me. Now what do I have to do?

T   Well, I want you to think about your own personal space. Then color the area in around yourself that shows your personal space.

F   I'm just going to draw a circle instead of coloring it in.

T   That's okay. The important thing is to try and show how close you feel comfortable with other people getting near to you.

F   There, that's my personal space.

T   So are you trying to show that you are comfortable with people getting really close to you?

F   NO! See how my arms are spread out and the circle still doesn't touch my hands.

T   Yep, I see that. So you don't like other people coming too close to you, huh?

F   I only like them to get close to me when I say it's okay.

T   So when you can be the boss of when people get close to you, it's okay, huh?

F   Yep.

T   Well at least if you are the boss then you can make sure no one is going to hurt you.

F   That's right.

T   I can understand that Freddy, but it's hard to learn to trust people if you always have to keep them away from you. Sounds like we need to keep helping you learn how to tell if other people can be trusted.

Clinical Impressions: It is easy to see that Freddy continues to show oppositional behavior. He resisted following directions, attempting to change the activity. Instead of just coloring in his personal space, he drew a circle. This is common behavior with traumatized children. As you could see, the therapist allowed Freddy to change the activity to fit his needs. It is important not to challenge oppositional children. You may end up engaging in a battle over directions rather than progressing into the activity. For some traumatized children, this is exactly what they want. It allows them to stay away from the pain of the trauma and be engaged in a "battle of wills."

The picture (see Illustration 4.1) reveals Freddy's need for control. He has unusually large hands and arms compared to the rest of his

Illustration 4.1.

body. This child does use his big hands and arms in a defensive and often assaultive manner. His arms are stretched out in such a way that it appears that he has a need to keep others away. Freddy's legs are two sticks without feet. He appears ungrounded and perhaps off balance.

Freddy shaded in the upper torso but left the bottom unshaded. Freddy was overweight. It is unclear whether he was attempting to cover up his large size or whether the bottom, unshaded oval part (which was added after he was done) was his large stomach just hanging out. It is also unclear if this added part was his sexual appendage, because he refused to discuss the drawing of his body. He would discuss only the boundary around him.

Ideally, it would be beneficial to engage the child in a conversation about body image in addition to the personal space, especially if there were questions regarding a specific part of the body, as there were here. This drawing and interactions reveal that this child is still in the beginning stage of recovery, and the prognosis is guarded.

Freddy continued to be defensive and resistant to anyone getting emotionally close to him. After more than 4 months of residential treatment, he was still in the early stages of building a therapeutic rapport with his therapist and other staff members.

❏ **Activity #24: Shane's Story**

Objective: To explore the definitions of appropriate and inappropriate social behaviors as they relate to the story presented.

This activity is designed to explore the definitions of appropriate and inappropriate social behaviors. The concept of personal and private space will be discussed. Again, due to inadequate "teaching," abused children are typically unaware or confused regarding the concept of appropriate social behaviors.

Children usually enjoy storytelling, and this can be a gentle way of exploring and learning uncomfortable concepts. However, stories may elicit underlying thoughts and feelings associated with prior abuse histories. Thus, while reading this story, it is important to be aware of both verbal and nonverbal cues the child may express.

Ages: This activity is appropriate for children ages 6 to 12, provided you read the story to children with reading difficulties. For these children, the questions also will need to be read, and the child can dictate the answers to you.

Materials Needed: Activity sheet and pencil, crayons, markers, and/or colored pencils.

Instructions: Instruct the child to read the story (if the child is unable to read, you will need to read it aloud) and answer the questions at the end of the story.

Processing: After reading the story, it is important to process feelings related to the story and other feelings that may have been elicited by the story. We have found it helpful to ask, "What are personal and private boundaries?" "What do you think of how Shane's father treated him?" "What did you think of how Shane's sister just walked in his room without asking?"

The following case example will illustrate how one physically and emotionally abused child processed this activity.

Case Example: *José*

Brief Case History: José is a 6½-year-old who was referred to the Partial Hospital Program due to difficulties handling his anger, difficulties with self-expression, jealousy toward his sister, rage episodes, and extremely poor interactive skills. At the time of his admission, José had just been returned to his mother's custody, who also had custody of his 3-year-old half-sister.

José had been in and out of his mother's care much of his life. This was primarily due to his mother's drug abuse and the frequent bouts of domestic violence between his mother and her boyfriend. The last time, José and his younger sister were removed from their mother's care, and the police were called due to a fight between José's mother and his sister's father.

On one such occasion, both José and his sister were in the kitchen when the adults started fighting. His mother was stabbed with a knife, and José tried to call 911 for help. On another occasion, pushing and shoving began, which then led to things being thrown, and José's sister was injured with a flying plate. Although the children were hurt during these altercations, their injuries were "accidental" in that the aggression was not directed at them. However, José's mother would frequently take out her anger and frustration on José. He would be hit with belts, shoes, her fists, and so on. His mother would also cuss at him and call him names when she was upset.

As previously stated, José had been in and out of his mother's care on several occasions. He had lived with his mother a total of approximately 2½ years out of his 6½ years. At one point, José lived with his maternal grandmother. Then he was placed in several foster homes, which was followed by a brief placement in an acute psychiatric unit of a hospital. Finally, he was placed in a RTC for several months prior to his eventual return to his mother's care.

The following example was taken from a session held with José when finishing up Phase I of his treatment. He was developing a fairly strong therapeutic relationship that was beginning to allow him to at least acknowledge that he had been mistreated. When José initially entered treatment, he continually denied that he had been hurt and/or mistreated.

Example of Activity #24

The session began with a discussion of José's weekend with his mom and sister. José then was told that we would be reading a story and discussing it. José was agreeable to the activity.

Due to his difficulties with paying attention for periods of time, the processing questions were discussed prior to reading the story. The story was then read to José because he was not at a functioning level where he could read it himself.

Therapist Well, José, what did you think of this story?
José It was good. Shane learned how to not get in as much trouble.
J   Tell me, José, how do you think Shane's father and sister violated or weren't respectful to his boundaries?
J   I don't understand what you mean.
T   Were Shane's father and sister being respectful to him?
J   No.
T   How were they disrespectful to Shane?
J   She was going in his room.
T   You mean his sister?
J   Uh huh. And his dad was drinking and getting really mad at him. He probably was hitting him.
T   Maybe. What do you think of what Shane's father and sister were doing?
J   It wasn't okay because it wasn't respecting other people's space.
T   How did Shane learn to be more respectful with his friends?

J He learned by his teacher. His teacher helped him use his words.

T What kinds of words do you think his teacher helped him to use?

J Well he probably learned to say, "May you please stop doing that?" when other kids were bugging him.

T That would be a good thing to say instead of getting mad and getting into a fight, huh? Can you think of any other words that Shane might be able to use?

J He could say, "May I please play with that?"

T That is a very respectful way of talking to someone. If you ask first instead of just taking, you are being very respectful.

J Uh huh. I'm learning how to be more respectful, aren't I?

T You sure are. You really have been working hard on being more respectful to other people. What do you think personal and private space means?

J Private space means not touching other people's private parts. Private stuff is with someone's body.

T That's right. What do you think someone's personal space means?

J I'm not sure. Does it mean like my bedroom?

T Yep, your bedroom could be your personal space. Personal space is an area that you think is your own. Your personal space could also be the area around you. Like when you are sitting, and that space that you feel more comfortable not having any-one come close to you. (demonstrated by physically moving closer to José and then moving back)

J Oh yeah, I get it.

T Anything else you want to tell me about the story? Have you ever had anything like this happen with you?

The remainder of the session was spent discussing various memo-ries José had regarding times when his mother hit him and would "get in his face."

Clinical Impressions: As you can see from this example, even children with speech and language deficits can work through this activity with the assistance of the therapist. When José did not understand what a word meant, he asked. This gave the therapist a chance to engage in a dialogue with him to further his understanding of the concepts. His questions allowed the therapist to assess just how far José had come in his therapy.

The story is brief and fairly general, which allows the child to interject his or her own issues. This was clear when José answered the first question with a comment that the dad was probably hitting Shane (the boy in the story). The story did not specifically state that at all. However, in José's life experiences, when caretakers were not sober, domestic violence was a common occurrence.

José had a history of just hitting rather than using his words to express his displeasure. It was interesting to have him give two examples of how to use words to express feelings, because this had been such a problem in the past.

José's answers seem to express his progress in therapy. Even with his language deficits, he has revealed tremendous growth in his ability to understand personal boundaries and the need to become more respectful of others.

❏ **Activity #25: The Private Triangle**

Objective: To begin to understand the concept of the *private triangle.*

This activity is designed to introduce the concept of the private triangle. The private triangle is the area on the body that includes the child's "private" parts. This is a concrete way of teaching the child how to define the area of the body that is most personal and needs the most protection.

On the front of the child, the triangle is actually inverted, extending from the shoulders, as the base, to just below the crotch, where the triangle connects. On the backside of the child, the triangle forms a base across the child's bottom and extends upward, connecting at the base of the neck.

Ages: This activity is designed for children ages 6 to 10 who do not have a disability that would impair them from physically participating.

Materials Needed: Activity sheet.

Instructions: Instruct the child to look at the pictures found on the activity sheet. Explain that he or she has a private triangle area on his or her body, just like everybody else.

Demonstrate how the child can form a triangular shape with his or her arms and hands, using the picture found on the activity sheet as an example. You will need to help the child visualize the private triangle on the backside, because that triangle cannot be made physically. Again, use the picture as an example. This activity generally is fun, because it allows the child to get up, move around, and be interactive.

Note: If the child is physically challenged, you can demonstrate the private triangle for him or her. Older children may think this is too "childish" for them; therefore, this activity may not be appropriate for 11- or 12-year-olds. You will be the best judge of that.

Processing: After working with the child on this activity by demonstrating the private triangle, it is important to follow up with questions to see if the child understands this concept. We have found it helpful to ask, "What does private triangle mean?" "Why is it important to know where your private triangle is?" "How does it feel to make your own private triangle?"

❏ Activity #26: Private Triangle—Dot to Dot

Objective: To continue exploring the concept of the private triangle.

This activity is designed to reinforce the concept of the private triangle (see explanation for Activity #25).

Ages: 6 to 10 years old. Older children may find this activity "childish."

Materials Needed: Activity sheet and pencil, crayons, and/or colored pencils.

Instructions: Instruct the child to connect the dots and color in the private triangle. Discuss the private triangle and the importance of it as the child is working on this activity. Then allow the child to color in the rest of the picture.

Processing: After the child completes the dot-to-dot picture, it is helpful to process with the child to assess the understanding of this concept. We have found it helpful to ask, "What is the private triangle?" "What is important about the private triangle?" "Tell me about your picture."

❑ **Activity #27: Private Triangle—Cut and Paste**

Objective: To continue understanding the concept of the private triangle.

This activity is designed to further support the concept of the private triangle. This activity will enable the child to actually cut out the triangular area and place it appropriately on the figure's body. For further explanation of the rationale for this concept, see Activity #25.

Ages: Children ages 6 to 10 years should have fun with this activity. The younger, developmentally delayed, or handicapped child who has problems with scissors may need assistance.

Materials Needed: Activity sheet; scissors; glue; crayons, colored pencils, and/or markers.

Instructions: Instruct the child to cut out the triangular shape at the bottom of the picture provided. After the shape has been cut out, tell the child to glue it on so that the private triangle is covered on the figure. Once the cutting and gluing have been completed, encourage the child to color in the picture.

You may want to encourage the child to color the private triangle area quite differently from the rest of the picture, clearly differentiating the private triangle from the rest of the figure's body.

Processing: After the child has completed this activity, it is important to process the activity with him or her by asking, "What is the difference between the private triangle and the rest of the figure's body?" "Tell me about your picture."

❑ Activity #28: My Private Triangle

Objective: To associate the concept of the private triangle to the child's own body.

This activity is designed to help the child assimilate the concept of the private triangle to the child's own body. This activity will also assist you in assessing the child's image of his or her overall body in perspective to his or her private areas.

Ages: This activity is designed for children ages 6 to 10 who are able to draw a human figure well enough so that the triangle can be drawn on the body. For younger or developmentally delayed children, your assistance may be needed.

Materials Needed: Activity sheet and pencils, crayons, markers, and/or colored pencils.

Instructions: Instruct the child to draw a picture of himself or herself and to draw a private triangle over the appropriate area on the child's portrait. It will be interesting to note what area the child perceives as the private area on his or her own body. The instruction should, therefore, be given in such a manner that the child is left with the decision of where to draw his or her own private triangle on the body. If the child draws only a head, encourage him or her to draw a stick figure.

Note: Older children, ages 11 and 12, may find this concept "childish." However, some developmentally delayed children will still enjoy this activity at 11 or 12 years.

Processing: After the child has completed the drawing, it important to process the drawing with him or her. We have found it helpful to ask, "Show me where your private triangle is on your picture." "Is this the same as the area on your own body?" "How do you feel about your private triangle?" "Has anyone ever not respected your private areas? Tell me about it."

PHASE II

Exploration of Trauma

5

Developing Trust and Being Safe

Children are born with the instinct to trust and a basic innocence, which makes them easy targets for abuse. When this trust is violated, the innocence of childhood is lost. Abuse shatters children's trust and violates their basic instincts and perceptions of others, leaving them emotionally vulnerable and making them targets for revictimization. They no longer feel "safe." If the abuser was the parent or another trusted adult figure, the sense of betrayal is even greater (Bolton & Bolton, 1987; Finkelhor & Browne, 1986; Herman, 1981; Malchiodi, 1990; Sgroi, 1982).

Finkelhor and Browne (1986) have proposed a model that can be used to understand the initial and long-term effects of child sexual abuse. The model includes four trauma-causing factors that they refer to as *traumagenic dynamics*—traumatic sexualization, stigmatization, betrayal, and powerlessness.

The betrayal dynamic refers to the sense of a betrayal of trust experienced by the child sexual abuse victim. Although Finkelhor and Browne attribute this dynamic to child sexual abuse, we have found that this sense of betrayal also can be found with victims of physical and emotional abuse or neglect.

Webb (1991) describes the betrayal dynamic in children as leading to difficulty in interpersonal relationships, which includes guardedness, suspiciousness, ambivalence, and choosing relationships in which one is exploited. In addition, antisocial attitudes and behaviors may evolve in response to the rage and anger associated with the sense of betrayal.

In addition to the betrayal dynamic mentioned above, the abused child often is stigmatized by negative statements made by the abuser. These children often are made to feel like they are the ones who are "crazy," and many times they are made to feel responsible for the inappropriate and abusive actions of others. It's not unusual for perpetrators to tell their victims things such as "You made me do it," "If you weren't so sexy . . .," "You made me angry," "You're stupid," "You're just like your father/mother."

The child's reality often is negated by such statements as "That's not true," "He/she wouldn't have done that," "You're lying," "You're just making it up." The internalization of these negative statements and judgments made by others, during or following child abuse, frequently produces guilt, shame, and self-blame (Briere, 1992; Courtois, 1988). Finkelhor and Browne (1986) refer to this in the stigmatization dynamic of their traumagenic model mentioned earlier. Webb (1991) lists self-deprecating behaviors, self-mutilating behaviors, and/or self-destructive behaviors as common manifestations of the stigmatization dynamic. The end result is abuse-related poor self-esteem (Briere, 1992).

Children who have had their trust and safety violated react to their environments in diverse ways. Some become hypervigilant, reacting to even the mildest stimulus. Others become apathetic, appearing not to care who or what intrudes their environment. Still others perceive any form of maltreatment as associated with danger or even, in some cases, fear of impending death (Conte, Briere, & Sexton, 1989). Therefore, the abused child must first learn what healthy trust is. This process begins with learning to trust oneself.

The goal of this chapter is to help the child understand trust and learn how to be "safe." Helping the child to establish trust and learning the dynamics of a "safe relationship" are essential objectives in trauma resolution work. The activities in this chapter are designed to assist children in attaining this goal.

Because the focus in this chapter is on trust and safety, the child may begin "testing" the limits of the relationship with you as his or her therapist. The child is "testing" to ensure that you will be a "safe" person, by maintaining a healthy balance between unconditional acceptance and limit setting. Therefore, maintaining this balance will be critical throughout your work with this child.

We have included a few case studies and examples of actual dialogue to help you in further understanding how some of these activities have been used in therapy sessions. As we have stated previously, it is important to engage in a thorough processing of each activity. Therefore, we have included a "Processing" section to assist you in your discussions with the child. These questions are general, so you may want to tailor-make questions to suit the individual needs of the child.

As the other chapters have indicated, the Activity Book includes a "Message to the Kids" section. This introduces the topic of the chapter to the child in more child-appropriate language. You may want to read this to the child you are working with or give it to him or her to read. The child can put this with the other "Messages" in his or her folder.

❑ Activity #29: Valerie's Story

Objective: To learn about the concept of feeling "safe" by reading about one girl's story.

This activity is designed to introduce the child to the concept of feeling safe. Children enjoy the medium of storytelling, and we have found this to be less threatening to children. Therefore, we have chosen to use a character that many abused/neglected children may identify with and have created a story about a girl's struggle with feeling safe.

Although this story was designed to be a simple introduction to the concept of safety, it may elicit a significant amount of discomfort, depending on the child's abusive background. If the child does exhibit or express signs of distress, this indicates a need for further intervention at this point. The child should be supported in exploring the cause(s) of the discomfort.

Ages: This activity is appropriate for children ages 6 to 12, provided you read the story to children with reading difficulties.

Materials Needed: Activity sheets and pencils, crayons, markers, and/or colored pencils.

Instructions: Instruct the child to read or listen to the story about Valerie. After reading the story, instruct the child to complete the questions. Process the questions with the child.

Note: For children with reading difficulties, the story and questions will need to be read, and the child then may dictate the answers to you.

Processing: After the child has finished reading the story or after the story has been read aloud, we have found it helpful to discuss the story by asking, "What do you think about the story?" "Tell me what being safe means to you." "Have there ever been times when you didn't feel safe? Why or why not?" "Tell me about your picture." (With older children, they may not wish to draw a picture but may want to discuss how this story relates to their own life experiences.)

Case Example: *Jamal*

Brief Case History: Jamal was a 9-year-old who was referred to the Partial Hospital Program due to exhibiting extremely poor social skills, being severely oppositional/defiant in both his home and school settings, experiencing gender confusion that included active "cross-dressing," and seeming to have cognitive problems.

Jamal was in his fourth foster placement since being removed from his maternal grandmother's care. He was removed when he was almost 4 years old. He was 8 to 9 months old when he was originally placed with her, following his mother's abandonment. It seems his biological mother simply packed up and moved to another state, leaving Jamal with his grandmother. His mother was apparently a heavy crack addict and used throughout her pregnancy.

Eventually, Jamal was removed from his grandmother's care by the state Child Protective Services. There had been several reports made by the neighbors of physical abuse and neglect. In addition, Jamal had been exhibiting highly sexualized behaviors, including frequent and/or obsessive masturbation, "humping" stuffed animals at day care, and dressing in girls' clothing.

Following his removal, reports were made that his grandmother was "running a house of prostitution" that was most frequented by "homeless" men. Also, it was reported that she was prostituting herself and selling heroin. His grandmother did admit that she would allow Jamal to be in unsupervised contact with these men.

Since Jamal's removal from his grandmother's custody at age 4, he has been placed in at least three other foster homes. At the time of his placement in the Partial Hospital Program, he was in his fourth foster home and had been there for almost a year.

In Jamal's current placement, he was reported as having set several fires, cross-dressing, masturbating frequently, encouraging other children in sexualized interactions, exhibiting severe aggression toward adults, having poor school performance, making threats of false reporting against adult helpers, and having poor communication and language skills.

Prior to Jamal's placement in the Partial Hospital Program, he had other therapeutic interventions. He had been in a therapeutic preschool program for well over a year, had several outpatient therapists, and had been placed with foster parents who were licensed as therapeutic.

In the Partial Hospital Program, Jamal was able to establish a relationship relatively quickly. This was probably in part due to the fact that he had previously had much intervention. It also may have been due to his attachment difficulties. Jamal seemed somewhat indiscriminate with his attachments, as do many children with reactive attachment difficulties.

The following example was taken from a session approximately 3 months into Jamal's treatment.

Example of Activity #29

The session began with a discussion about Jamal's sense of feeling safe. He was very clear that he did not feel safe most of the time. He then was told that a story about one little girl's sense of safety was going to be read and discussed. The story was then read and the following discussion was held.

Therapist What did you think about the story, Jamal?
Jamal It was all right. I kind of feel sad for Valerie.
T   How come . . . why do you feel sad for her?
J   'Cause she didn't feel very safe.
T   Yeah, it is sad when kids don't feel safe. What do you think being safe means to Valerie?
J   It means like her mom loves her.
T   How do you think her mom would show her that she loves her?
J   By her not doing nasty things to her brother.
T   You mean her mom wouldn't do nasty things to her brother.
J   (Nodded)
T   Does nasty things mean private touching? (This information already had been obtained in previous sessions. This is not new information.)
J   (Nodded)
T   Yeah, if adults are going to be safe with kids, they wouldn't do private touching stuff. How do you think Valerie's mother could show her that she was going to be safe with her?
J   By showing her respect.
T   And how do you think her mother could show her that she respected her?
J   By not hitting her with a belt.
T   Yeah, adults that respect kids don't hit with belts. I don't think they would hit at all, do you?
J   Nope. My granny used to hit me. She hit me with a belt, her hand, shoes, all kinds of stuff.
T   I know. . . . I'm really sorry you were treated that way. You never deserve to be treated like that. What does being safe mean to you?
J   Not touching other people's space or privates.

T   So you know people are safe when they don't get into your
    space or try to touch your privates, huh?
J   Uh huh.
T   When do you feel safest, Jamal?
J   When I am around grown-ups.
T   So you feel like grown-ups are safe.
J   Well, I don't know if all of them are safe.
T   How can you tell when a grown-up is safe?
J   I watch them. If they ask me about feelings, then I know they
    are safe.
T   So when adults talk to you about your feelings, then you think
    they are safer people.
J   Uh huh.
T   Do you think Valerie's mom talked to her about her feelings
    very much?
J   Nope. I feel sorry for her.
T   Yeah, it is sad when kids don't feel safe. Would you like to draw
    a picture of Valerie.
J   Yeah, can I draw it on a separate piece of paper?
T   Sure you can Jamal.

The remainder of the session was spent with Jamal drawing his
picture, and then it was discussed.

Clinical Impressions: Clearly, this child has been severely traumatized
by his chaotic, troubled, early childhood experiences. This is seen
by how quickly Jamal interjects his own abuse experiences when
processing "Valerie's Story." He appears stuck in his fears of being
revictimized. This most likely has been caused by repeated abuses
by adults around him.

Jamal's readiness to explore his traumatic past is reflective of
children who have been engaged in prior therapy. However, he
reveals little evidence of good boundary development in his overt
willingness to discuss painful, past abuses in detail, even before
developing a therapeutic rapport.

Jamal acts as a reporter of feelings rather than a child who is
experiencing the feelings associated with trauma. This is common
with children who suffer from reactive attachment disorders. This

denotes the damage that has been done to Jamal's sense of self. Briere (1992) refers to some victims as suffering from other-directedness, meaning that the child is dependent on understanding the demands of others rather than being more self-directed. The child becomes hypervigilant and is always anticipating what others expect of them. This seems to be the case with Jamal. He is so tuned to what is going on with others that he does not focus well on his own needs.

This activity highlights Jamal's ongoing therapeutic needs that include development of healthier boundaries, allowing him to experience his feelings associated with his traumatic past and learning to trust himself so he is better able to take care of his own needs.

In regard to the cross-dressing, Jamal's grandmother used to dress him in girls' clothing. It is unclear whether this is a gender/identity issue or part of his past learned behavior. Identity confusion is part of the diagnosis of Borderline Personality Disorder, commonly found in adults abused as children. Therefore, this could be an early indication of an emerging personality disorder.

It is interesting to note that a few weeks after Jamal was placed in the Partial Hospital Program, he ceased the cross-dressing behavior. Perhaps Jamal felt safer and more nurtured and did not need to use old behaviors to satisfy his sense of emptiness.

❏ **Activity #30: My Safe Places**

Objective: To discuss where the child feels safe.

This activity is designed to allow children to brainstorm about the places where they feel safe. It is important to determine where children feel safe or unsafe in their environment. This activity may assist in uncovering specifics regarding abuse history. You may find that the child does not feel very safe in his or her environment. If that is the case, you may want to explore this further, because this *may* be an indicator of an abusive experience in this environment.

It is important to note that the abused child is often in a state of denial and may not be willing, or is unable, to identify safe or unsafe places. As the child works through these activities, it is hoped that he or she will develop a sense of safety that will enable the child to engage in the healing process.

Ages: This activity is designed for children ages 6 to 12.

Materials Needed: Activity sheet (extra sheets may be needed) and pencils, crayons, markers, and/or colored pencils.

Instructions: Instruct the child to think about various places he or she feels safe. Then instruct the child to list and/or draw the places he or she feels safe. In addition to the following processing questions, you may find it helpful to discuss the child's feelings about safety as he or she completes this activity.

Note: The older child may want to both draw and list safe places, but younger or developmentally delayed children may choose to list or dictate places that feel safe if their drawing abilities are not very well developed.

Processing: After completing this activity, it is important to ask the child about his or her safe places. We have found it helpful to ask, "Tell me about your safe places." "What makes these places safe for you? Why?" "How did you feel while you were listing and/or drawing your safe places?"

❑ Activity #31: My Safest Place

Objective: To determine where the child feels safest.

This activity is designed to determine where children feel the safest in their environment. Although a child may list several places that he or she feels safe, it is important to identify the one place that a child feels the safest for many reasons. First, it will assist in assessing the child's reality base (i.e., does the child choose a place he or she has been *told* is safe or where he or she truly *is* "safe"?).

This activity will also help determine whether the child has the skills to differentiate between his or her own level of comfort with the sense of personal safety. For example, although the child may have identified several places that feel safe, he or she may identify one particular place that feels the safest.

In addition, having the child identify the place where he or she feels the safest can assist in the therapeutic process. By simply sharing this place with you, the child is acknowledging a sense of trust on some level. Also, you will be able to reference this place as you proceed through the process of healing.

Ages: Although this activity is designed for children ages 6 to 12, the younger or developmentally delayed child may choose to dictate something about his or her safest place.

Materials Needed: Activity sheet and pencils, crayons, markers, and/or colored pencils.

Instructions: Instruct the child to think about all of the safe places he or she listed in Activity #30 (you may need to review them together). Then have the child choose the place where he or she feels the safest. After the child has made a selection, instruct him or her to write about or draw the place.

Processing: After the activity is completed, have the child tell you about his or her safest place by asking, "Tell me about the place where you feel the safest." "What makes this place safe to you?" "What makes this place safer to you than the other places you listed?"

Case Example: *Monica*

Brief Case History: Monica was an 11-year-old Hispanic-Anglo girl who was the only child of her adopted parents. She had been in this family unit since she was 4 years old. She was adopted when she was 6½ years old.

Monica was removed form her biological parents when she was 3 years old. The state took legal custody of Monica after several reports of abuse and neglect. Once in the state's custody, it was substantiated that Monica had suffered severe sexual abuse that left

Monica with permanent internal scarring and damage to her bladder. The multiple scars on her body also indicated multiple incidents of physical abuse as well. Records also indicated that Monica lived in an environment in which there were violent fights between her biological parents, who also frequently abused substances.

After Monica was removed from her biological parents, she was placed in a state facility for children who were awaiting adoption and/or other placements. Monica was in this placement for several months because she was a difficult youngster to place in a home setting. At this early age, Monica was already showing signs of severe emotional difficulties. She would frequently throw temper tantrums lasting for hours; attempt to bite, kick, hit, pinch, and spit at other children and adults; and isolate herself from others by sitting and facing the wall any time anyone would attempt to interact with her. In addition, Monica had an extremely difficult time sleeping and would stay awake for hours and have tantrums.

Monica's adopted parents met her in the state's facility for children; her adopted mother volunteered at the facility. Monica's adopted mother immediately "fell in love" with her and with the idea of "turning this angry little girl around." Once in her "new" home, Monica quickly showed her adoptive parents that parenting her was not going to be an easy task. Monica spent many hours hunched under the furniture in the house, refused to go to bed at night, threw temper tantrums that would last hours, became physically assaultive, and refused to allow her new parents to comfort or cuddle with her. These behaviors continued over a long period of time, with the intensity decreasing over the years.

Monica and her adoptive parents began receiving family therapy approximately 5 years after she was placed in their home. In addition, Monica was placed on several different kinds of medication to assist her with her ongoing behavioral problems. These interventions did not seem to assist Monica and/or her parents, and her behaviors continued to worsen. Eventually, Monica was referred for more intense treatment and was placed in a 3-hour Partial Hospital Program.

At the time of her admission, Monica was continuing to exhibit difficulties in all of her settings. In her public school placement, she was described as having no friends, frequently getting into fistfights with other children, refusing to go to school, being extremely oppositional with teachers and other authority figures, being expelled, and experiencing poor academic performance.

In her home, Monica was completely out of control. She would yell and scream at her parents. She was physically out of control, which included punching and kicking holes in walls and doors, throwing things, hitting her parents, cussing and swearing, refusing to do the simplest of tasks, running away from home, and having frequent temper tantrums that would include regressed and "babyish" behaviors.

It took a significantly long period of time to develop even the slightest amount of trust with Monica. It was several weeks before Monica would talk in a group setting and/or play with the other children in the Partial Hospital Program. In one-on-one sessions, Monica would discuss her day-to-day activities on a surface level and would quickly "shut down" if one attempted to probe any further. Eventually, Monica did develop some trust with her therapeutic team and began working on issues that she was experiencing in her day-to-day life.

The following example was from a session that was held a few months into Monica's treatment. It is obvious from Monica's picture and the difficulty she had in discussing why this was her safest place that she continued to struggle with the issue of trust. Monica's difficulties in developing a sense of trust made it very difficult to assist her through her traumatic experiences.

Example of Activity #31

At the beginning of the session, the importance of feeling safe and what it meant to be safe were discussed. Monica was then asked to draw a picture of the place or places where she felt the safest. After Monica drew her picture, Monica and her therapist discussed what she had drawn and why she had chosen this place.

Therapist So Monica, whose house did you draw as your safest place?

Monica This is my Grandma's house; here I'll write it on my picture so that you won't forget.

T Which Grandma's house is this, your Mom's or your Dad's mom?

M This is my Nana (Grandmother)—my Mom's mom.

T What makes your Grandma's house feel the safest to you? Is it the house itself or the people that are there or what?

M It's the people that are there. I always feel safe when I go to my Nana's house.

T What do the people do or don't do that makes you feel safe?

M Well first of all my Nana helps me.

T How does your Nana help you?

M When she doesn't want me to do something she tells me instead of yelling at me.

T So when people yell at you, you don't feel very safe.

M Right. And my Nana will explain things to me that I don't know how to do.

T It sounds like your Nana takes the time to make sure that you understand things, and then you don't have to feel so frustrated. It also sounds like you let your Nana explain things to you without getting defensive or mad. Are there other things that make you feel safe at your Nana's house?

M Yeah. My Nana talks to me. She makes me happy and makes me laugh. She will tell me things in Spanish that people say in English. It's like we have our own private jokes.

T It sounds like your Nana is very special to you. It seems like not only do you trust her but that you have a friendship with her.

M I do trust her. My Nana never yells at me and she doesn't ever tell me to get out (of her house).

T So your Nana would never push you away and tell you that she doesn't want you around. Are there other reasons you feel so safe at your Nana's house?

M Well, my Tia (aunt) is there, too, and she helps me talk about my feelings. My Tio (uncle) is there and he always gives me food to eat.

T So it's not just your Nana that makes her house safe for you. It sounds like it is all the people that live there. Your Tia and Tio help you with your feelings and give you things to eat. It seems like you feel safe with them because they take the time to give you the things every kid needs, like to be listened to and to be fed.

M My Nana also goes for walks with me, she will listen to me no matter what I have to say. She also shares things with me without me having to ask (like part of her candy bar).

T Boy, I'm glad to hear that you feel so safe at your Nana's house, Monica. It seems like you really know the things that other people can do in order for you to feel safe with them.

M Uh huh.

T One important thing that you've said several times is that you need people to listen to you without getting mad and start yelling at you, no matter what has happened. It also seems like it is important for you to be around people that will help you talk about your feelings.

M Like my Nana.

T I'm glad you have people in your family that you feel safe with. Maybe we can start working on paying attention to other people like your Mom and Dad to see if they can do the same kinds of things.

M Okay.

T We might have to tell them sometime what things are important to you so that you feel safe with them too.

The session ended soon after this.

Clinical Impressions: The picture drawn by Monica is actually very immature (see Illustration 5.1). The barren gray color that surrounds the house depicts a sense of gloom. Clearly, she doesn't feel too safe outside the house. On the other hand, the house doesn't offer any sense of warmth. The handle to the front door is depicted as heavy and suggests a need to possibly keep others out. It connotes a continuing struggle with trust issues.

Monica makes it clear that she still struggles with trusting her adopted parents. It is interesting to note that the Nana, who she feels so close to, is suffering from Alzheimer's. As the Nana progresses in her disease, Monica will most likely feel abandoned, recreating her life story.

Building a trusting relationship is critical in this child's therapy. Monica is fearful of forming a close relationship and seems to set

my Grandma's House

Illustration 5.1.

herself up for failure. Unfortunately, her inability to fully understand her Nana's condition will add to this problem, because she
looks to her for understanding and closeness.

This activity suggests that Monica may need to continue with
trust building before she is able to progress into the exploration
phase of recovery. She still needs to build a close therapeutic bond
with her outpatient therapist.

As so sadly happens in some of these cases, the therapist working
with her in the Early Childhood Program was replaced by a new
outpatient therapist. This will clearly make it more difficult for this
child to progress into the exploration phase of her recovery. She will
need to form a therapeutic rapport with her new therapist in order
to "trust" this new person.

❏ **Activity #32: Unsafe Places**

Objective: To identify and discuss the places where the child feels unsafe.

This activity is designed to encourage children to identify and explore the places where they feel unsafe. Just as it is important to have children identify places where they feel safe, it is equally important to help children identify places where they feel unsafe. As stated earlier, the child may feel unsafe within certain environments. It is important to check this out, because it may indicate where possible abuse occurred.

Ages: This activity is designed for ages 6 to 12.

Materials Needed: Activity sheet (extra paper may be needed) and pencils, crayons, markers, and/or colored pencils.

Instructions: Instruct the child to think about various places he or she feels unsafe. Then instruct the child to list and/or draw the place(s) that do not feel safe. If the child refuses or states that there is no place he or she feels unsafe, encourage the child to draw or list place(s) that are the least comfortable for him or her.

Note: As mentioned in the previous activity, younger children or developmentally delayed children may prefer to dictate something about where they feel unsafe.

Processing: After the activity is completed, it is helpful to process the activity by asking, "Tell me about your unsafe place(s)." "What makes these places unsafe for you? Why?" "How did you feel while you were listing/drawing your unsafe place(s)?" "Which place felt the most unsafe?"

❏ Activity #33: Tommy's Story

Objective: To process the concept of trust through storytelling.

This activity is designed to introduce the child to the concept of trust. This story is about a child's struggle with an abusive older brother. Although it is not as threatening as other examples may be, some children still may react against the idea of trust in a caretaker or other person in their environment. If a child does exhibit signs of distress, this indicates further intervention. The child should be assisted in processing his or her feelings.

Ages: This activity is appropriate for children ages 6 to 12, provided you read the story to children with reading difficulties.

Materials Needed: Activity sheets and pencils, crayons, markers, and/or colored pencils.

Instructions: Instruct the child to read or listen to the story about Tommy. After reading this story, instruct the child to complete the questions and draw the picture. Process the given questions with the child.

Note: For children with reading difficulties, the story and questions may need to be read and the child can dictate the answers to you.

Processing: After reading the story, it is best to discuss the story and process how the child felt about it. We have found it helpful to ask, "What do you think about the story?" "Tell me what trust means to you." "Have there ever been people whom you felt you could not trust? Why or why not?" "Is there anyone you feel you can trust? Why or why not?" "Tell me about your picture." (Older children may not choose to draw a picture. They may prefer to discuss how their own life experiences compare with the story.)

❏ **Activity #34: People I Trust**

Objective: To continue processing and learning about the concept of trust.

This activity is designed to further explore the concept of trust. It is hoped that the child will be able to associate the abstract concept of trust in a more concrete fashion with people he or she trusts.

The word *trust* is such a common word used in our society that children lose the concept of what underlies this word. The media tend to overuse this word. Therefore, it's not surprising that children also misunderstand this word, which can place them at risk.

Children who have been abused often have been abused by the person they are supposed to trust. Many times, this person is left "in charge" of the child or assumes some kind of power over the child within the child's environment. Children become confused by what they hear about trust and what they experience by people who misuse their trust.

Ages: Children ages 6 to 12 should have very few problems with this activity.

Materials Needed: Activity sheet (extra paper may be needed) and pencils, crayons, markers, and/or colored pencils.

Instructions: Instruct the child to think about the person(s) who he or she trusts. Then tell the child to draw a picture of the person(s) on the activity sheet.

Note: The older, more mature child most likely will be more detailed in his or her picture and may even depict the person(s) engaged in an activity.

Processing: After the child completes the drawing(s), it is important to discuss the drawing(s) by asking, "Tell me about your drawing." "What makes you think you can trust this person(s)?" "How do you feel about this person(s)? Why?"

❏ Activity #35: Broken Trust

Objective: To identify ways that trust can be broken.

This activity is designed to allow the child to identify ways that trust can be broken. It is intended to be less threatening to the child because it asks the child to give general ways that trust is violated. However, this activity may elicit powerful feelings, because the child may associate specific acts perpetrated on him or her while verbalizing general ways that trust can be violated.

Although this activity is designed to elicit general ways trust can be violated in a generic sense, many children may find internal dynamics taking over. Therefore, you may observe behaviors that reflect this turmoil. Be aware of this and be prepared! It is important to attempt to keep the child focused on the general aspects of trust violations rather than getting into the specifics of the child's experience, because that is covered in the next activity.

Ages: This activity is designed for children ages 6 to 12 who have a general concept of trust that has been violated.

Materials Needed: Activity sheet and pencils, crayons, markers, and/or colored pencils.

Instructions: Instruct the child to draw or list different ways trust can be broken. You may find that you will need to assist the child to organize his or her thoughts during this activity. One fairly effective method in helping the child to do this is to review the previous activities that specifically address ways the child does trust others. Then take this information and ask the child to determine how his or her trust with this person(s) *could be* violated.

Note: If the child has difficulty writing or drawing, he or she may choose to dictate the responses.

Processing: After completing this activity, it is important to discuss the child's answers by asking, "Tell me about your picture(s) or list."

"Have other people broken your trust in them? How?" "How does it feel to have your trust broken? Why?"

Case Example: *Marty*

Brief Case History: Marty was a 6-year-old who was living in a group home when he was placed in the Partial Hospital Program. This was at least the fourth placement in the foster care system for Marty in his 6 years. Marty was the middle of five children in his biological family. His older brother was also in the foster care system. His younger siblings were placed back with their mother once again.

Marty and his siblings had been removed from their home for a multitude of reasons. The first couple of times the older boys were removed, it was due to neglect. The third removal came after the boys disclosed to their day care worker that their father had been sexually abusing them. Marty was only 3 at the time. It seemed that his father "framed" the sexual interactions in a gamelike way, which has caused Marty a great deal of turmoil. Marty continued to excuse or discount his abusive experiences, because his "Daddy was only playing a game."

The last removal occurred after Marty's mother had become very upset and angry with the children due to their lack of cooperation. Their biological father was out of the home and the mother had to raise the children on her own. By this time, both Marty and his brother were out of control most of the time. They had received few services following their disclosure. The final event causing their removal came after the mother grabbed one of the boy's hair and pushed his head against the wall, causing his nose to bleed. All of the children were removed at this time and placed in foster care. After a few months of therapy, the younger children were allowed to return home; however, Marty and his older brother remained out of the home.

In exploring Marty's family background, it was apparent that physical and sexual abuse went back several generations. Both his mother and father had an extremely difficult time acknowledging that their actions were somehow inappropriate.

Eventually, Child Protective Services decided the parental rights should be severed due to the lack of progress. The mother was unable to understand her role in her children's abuse. Severance was based on the lack of development of appropriate parenting skills and the mother's and the stepfather's inability to control their own anger.

The following example was taken from a session that occurred several weeks after Marty found out that he would not be returning home. He finally had pulled himself together behaviorally so that he could continue in his trauma work. Prior to his finding out that he would not be returning home, Marty had done a great deal of trauma recovery work regarding specific abusive experiences he had endured in his short lifetime.

Example of Activity #35

This activity was taken from a session approximately 8 months into Marty's treatment. He was going to be moving to a foster-adoptive home following the court's decision to sever his parents' rights.

Therapist Marty, I know that you are a little bit scared to be moving again. So I thought today we could talk about trust.

Marty I am a lot scared about moving. I don't know why I can't just go home.

T Well, you know the judge said Mom needed to learn how to not take her angry feelings out on you, like yelling at you during visits.

M I know. I just wish she wouldn't.

T I wish she wouldn't, too, that way you wouldn't have to feel so scared. Today I want you to think about reasons you trust people and reasons you don't.

M That's easy for me. . . . I know a lot of ways people can break trust.

T I bet you do, because you've met a lot of people in your lifetime. Maybe today we can make a poster about trust.

M Then other kids could look at it.

T That's right. Maybe your poster could help other kids to keep themselves safer. Let's put "Trust can be broken by . . ." at the top.

M Okay.

T   You can tell me ways you think trust can be broken or you can draw pictures.

M   I'll just tell you, but you can write, okay?

T   Okay. What's the first way you can think of that trust sometimes gets broken?

M   By parents hitting you.

T   Okay, how else can trust be broken?

M   Kids biting you.

T   Kids biting you, that's an interesting one. What do you mean by kids biting?

M   Well kids biting other kids or when a kid bites an adult when they are holding you.

T   Oh, that makes sense now. How else can trust be broken?

M   Parents making you have to sleep.

T   I don't understand what you mean by this.

M   You know, like not letting you get up at night when you have to go to the bathroom.

T   So like when you ask to go to the bathroom, your parents would say "no." You would have to stay in your bed?

M   Yeah, and by parents locking you in your room when you are sleeping.

T   Oh, so that's another new way, huh?

M   Yup. My mom used to lock me in my room when I'd be asleep. And when I would wake up the door would be locked. Then I would have to stay in my room for a really long time. I didn't like it when she did that.

T   I can't say that I blame you. I don't think I would like to wake up and be locked in either. Do you want to add anything else to your poster?

M   People being rude. And people being mean.

T   What do you mean by people being mean?

M   Like grown-ups hitting you with a belt. And when they yell at you, you can't trust them.

T   Do you want that to be a separate one? Number seven?

M   Uh huh. My poster has a lot of numbers, huh?

T   Yes it does. Are you finished or do you want to add more?

M   Well, can we play for a while and if I think of more I'll let you know. I want to play that bowling game.

T   Sure, we can do that.

As we were playing the game, Marty was talking about his new school starting and about missing his special friend. This was a person who would come on the weekends to take him for outings. However, he had been on vacation for the past 3 weeks and had not called Marty.

M Oh, I just thought of another one. Will you add it to the list?

T Sure, what did you think of?

M People saying they will call and they don't.

T Yeah, that kind of feels like broken trust, doesn't it? Maybe you can talk to Bill (his special friend) about how you wished he would have called you over his vacation.

M Okay . . . the last thing is, people making promises and they don't keep them.

T So that's the last thing you want to put on your poster?

M Yup, but if I think of more on another day I will just tell you, okay, and you can write it down. Now, can we finish bowling?

Clinical Impressions: It is obvious that Marty is very aware of how trust can be broken. This is based on his own experiences of various violations of trust directed at him. Interestingly, Marty does not seem to blame himself for his mother's abuse. He states clearly that she is to blame. This is unusual in that many abused children take on the blame for the abuse inflicted on them (as his brother does).

For a 6-year-old, Marty has an advanced ability to conceptualize trust and how someone violates this trust. Marty's sensitivity to his special friend's absence and lack of contact during this time may be indicative of hypervigilance. He seems keenly aware of any changes in his environment. This hypervigilance is common for abused children who are suffering symptoms of posttraumatic stress.

Marty did an excellent job in processing this activity. He was able to list and explore all the different ways he felt his trust has been broken. The activity itself was concrete enough that it did not seem to put Marty into "emotional overload" while still allowing him to confront some of his issues with his parents directly.

One way Marty seems to keep himself from being overwhelmed is to compartmentalize or distance himself from his feelings. He did this throughout the session by engaging in the activity and then switching to the bowling game. At this point in his treatment, this appears to be a functional coping strategy. However, this may produce difficulties in other settings, such as school when he is frustrated with academic tasks and is restricted from switching activities, to distance himself from his feelings.

Marty needs to continue exploring his trauma and feelings associated with his abuse history. It is hoped that with an empathic therapist he will allow himself to process these difficult feelings and learn more positive coping skills rather than distancing himself from his feelings.

❏ Activity #36: People I Don't Trust

Objective: To identify and discuss the person(s) the child does not trust.

This activity is designed to allow the child to identify and discuss the person(s) with whom the child feels uncomfortable and has a lack of trust. It is important for the child to be able to verbalize his or her feelings and the reasons for these feelings, thus breaking the "code of silence" and the fear so many abused children operate under.

You may find this activity to be very difficult for the abused child. For the child to complete this activity successfully, he or she may have to break this code of silence. It is difficult to anticipate just what a child has been told by the perpetrator to keep him or her quiet. Therefore, it is important to process carefully with the child how he or she feels while working on this activity. Also, it is important not to make judgments about what the child tells you.

Another critical aspect of the child revealing the abuser is the therapist's duty to report. The person identified by the child is a possible abuser and must be reported to the proper authorities. You should familiarize yourself with the child abuse reporting laws in your state.

Ages: This activity is designed for children ages 6 to 12.

Materials Needed: Activity sheet and pencils, crayons, markers, and/or colored pencils.

Instructions: Instruct the child to draw a picture of a person(s) who is not trusted. In addition to the processing questions below, you might want to process the child's feelings while he or she is drawing the picture(s).

Note: The child who has been traumatized severely may choose not to draw the perpetrator at this point due to intense emotional feelings. If drawing the actual picture is too difficult, the child may be able to simply list the person or people who are not trusted and/or who have caused harm.

Processing: After the child has completed this activity, it is important to discuss who the child does not trust by asking, "Tell me about your drawing(s)." "Why can't you trust that person(s)?" "How did you feel while drawing this picture? Why?" "How do you feel about this person(s)? Why?"

❏ **Activity #37: Safety Rules**

Objective: To develop rules that will assist in safeguarding against experiencing any future abuse.

This activity is designed to assist the child in developing a set of rules that will assist him or her in safeguarding against experiencing any future abuse. Developing a set of rules to keep safe and to keep others safe, as well as internalizing these rules, is imperative to the abused child's healing process. Therefore, this process will need to be repeated and reviewed as the child progresses through this workbook.

Ages: Children of all ages are able to participate in this activity, because it is a cooperative endeavor between you and the child.

Materials Needed: Activity sheet and pencils, crayons, markers, and/or colored pencils.

Instructions: Instruct the child to read or listen to the listed rules. Then instruct the child to draw or list three additional ways to keep himself or herself safe. Encourage an open discussion of ways to keep safe. If the child comes up with more than three additional rules, he or she should be reinforced for the added effort. Refrain from giving the child "your" ideas and also make sure the child's rules are appropriate in keeping him or her safe.

Note: Children are exposed to all sorts of rules at school, home, and so on; therefore, this is not a new concept. However, coming up with ways to keep himself or herself safe may be a new concept and may take a lot of discussion.

Processing: After the child completes the list, it is important to discuss the rules with him or her. We have found it helpful to ask, "How do you feel about the rules listed?" "Which rule do you feel is the safest? Why?" "Tell me about your rules." "How will these rules keep you safe?"

6

Secrets

It is often said that we are only as sick as our secrets. For most abused children, silence becomes a survival mechanism. Maintaining this silence adds to children's underlying feelings of guilt and shame, which increase the likelihood that the abuse will continue unnoticed or unreported.

Once trust is established, it is necessary to begin uncovering the hidden secrets. This is a very difficult and frightening process for most abused children, because the pressure to keep the secret is experienced psychologically as fear (Burgess & Holmstrom, 1978). Many children have been threatened or coerced to maintain silence. Often, these children are threatened with abandonment or rejection with comments such as "If you tell, I'll kill you," "If you tell, mommy and daddy will get divorced," "If you tell, your parents won't love you," "If you tell, you'll get in trouble." Other children have difficulty breaking the silence for fear they will not be believed or may be blamed for the abuse.

Burgess and Holmstrom (1978) refer to the dominant-subordinate role as another reason why children remain silent. Children are in the subordinate role in most situations, with the exception of peer-related interactions. Therefore, they often view this authority figure as setting the standard of what is right and wrong (i.e., if the adult does it, it must be right).

Another problem unique to little children is the communication barrier that naturally exists. Children often have difficulty verbalizing in adult language their experiences. It is highly unlikely that a young child will go up to an adult and explain in meaningful language exactly what happened. For one thing, if the abuser has approached the child in a nonthreatening manner, the child may not realize the behavior was "wrong."

Gil (1991) points out that even when spared overt threats, many children seem to sense the secrecy of family violence or sexual abuse. They may not feel they should talk about family matters. This is often conditioned over time.

Abused children typically need to know the difference between secrecy and privacy. It is important for children to understand the need for privacy, which can be empowering. However, children required to keep secrets feel burdened by this task, leaving them with an overwhelming sense of helplessness.

Children often confuse secrecy and privacy. In fact, it is not uncommon for abused children to say that they cannot talk about something that happened to them because it is private. These children need to sort out the difference between feeling empowered to share the secret that has kept them alienated from others and the right to privacy, such as using the bathroom or requesting a quiet time alone.

These children need a warm, nurturing, and safe environment in order to share their painful secrets. Talking about the abuse history is vital in the recovery process. However, these children need to understand that it is not necessary to share their secrets with everyone. Because abused children typically have a problem with appropriate boundaries, they sometimes indiscriminately share information. This may leave them vulnerable to revictimization, blame by others who do not fully understand child abuse and its effects, or criticism by their peers.

The goal of this chapter is to assist children in revealing their secrets and breaking their silence. The activities in this chapter are designed to assist the child in identifying, disclosing, and processing "secrets." Although children's reactions to disclosure vary considerably, a recent study by Berliner and Conte (1995) suggests that most children felt that disclosing their victimization was a "good" thing. However, this can also be a very painful process for the abused child.

During this period, children may again "act out" their conflicts, which may appear in the form of regressive or aggressive behaviors. This can be quite disconcerting to the therapist or other people involved with the child's treatment. It is important to support the child as he or she begins to process the "secrets" that have been "locked up" for so long. In addition to the activities outlined in this chapter, play therapy has been found to be an excellent therapeutic tool in processing traumatic events (Gil, 1991; Webb, 1991).

A few case studies and specific examples of some of the activities in this chapter are provided to further your understanding of how some of these activities have been used in actual therapy situations. We hope this helps you in your work with abused children.

Before beginning this chapter, you may want to have the child read the "Message to the Kids" for this chapter, found in the Activity Book. This will give a brief introduction to "Secrets." The child can put this with the other activities he or she has completed.

❑ Activity #38: Samantha's Story

Objective: To begin discussing the concept of secrets through storytelling.

This activity is designed to introduce the child to the concept of secrets and help the child differentiate between safe and unsafe secrets. It is normal for children to tell secrets as part of their play. However, for the abused child, secrets pose a confusing dilemma.

Although this story was designed to help the child become aware that there are different kinds of secrets, it may trigger memories or feelings of the child's own abuse history. You, as the therapist, need to be acutely aware of the child's body language, statements made, and behavioral changes. These may be "red flags" that the child is struggling with thoughts, feelings, or secrets that need to be addressed.

Ages: This activity is appropriate for children ages 6 to 12, provided you read the story to children with reading difficulties.

Materials Needed: Activity sheet and pencils.

Instructions: Instruct the child to read or listen to the story of Samantha. After reading the story, instruct the child to complete the questions related to the story. Process the questions with the child.

Note: For children with reading difficulties, the story and questions will need to be read and the child can dictate the answers to you.

Processing: After the story has been read, it is important to process the story with the child. Children seem to enjoy discussing various aspects of the story and may interject some of their own history during the discussion. We have found it helpful to ask, "What do you think about the story?" "What is the difference between safe and unsafe secrets?" "Give me an example of a safe secret and an unsafe one." "How did you feel about Samantha's secret?" "Have you ever had a secret that you thought you shouldn't tell?"

Case Example: *Julie*

Brief Case History: Julie was a 9½-year-old who was living in a foster home and attending public school. She was placed in the 3-hour Partial Hospital Program due to her out-of-control behaviors in her foster home and difficulties in her classroom at school.

When Julie was initially placed in treatment, part of the goal was to try and avoid yet another disruption in placement for her. Julie already had been in three other foster placements in the year she was in the state's custody.

Julie was the youngest of two girls—both currently were in the state's custody due to allegations that they had been sexually abused and neglected. Prior to being placed in the foster care system, Julie and her sister lived with their paternal grandmother.

Julie's parents had been divorced, and her father was given custody of both girls. It seems there were questions of the mother's mental stability at the time of the divorce. She later relinquished her rights and moved to another state.

Julie's father served in the military, and instead of the girls moving abroad with him, he left them in the care of his mother. It was here that the girls began disclosing the sexual abuse they had suffered at the hands of their father. Although Julie's grandmother initially reported her son to the authorities, when he returned from his overseas assignment she began to deny the validity of their reports. She eventually allowed the girls to have contact with their father once again. It was then that the girls were placed in the legal custody of the state.

Shortly after Julie and her sister were taken into the state's care, their father was court-marshalled by the military because he had written several thousand dollars' worth of bad checks. He was sentenced to 7 years in military prison, and his parental rights were severed.

Julie's grandmother did not want custody of the children, and there were questions of her ability to keep them safe; thus Julie and her sister remained in the state's custody and were legally free to be adopted. At the time of Julie's placement in the Partial Hospital Program, both girls were awaiting homes in which they could be adopted.

When Julie was initially placed into the Partial Hospital Program, she frequently argued with her foster mother, and the arguments began to escalate into physical confrontations. She also was described as being very "sneaky" (i.e., Julie would get up in the middle of the night and take food from the kitchen; she would then find various places in her bedroom to hoard the food). Julie's foster mother also reported that there were frequent episodes of lying.

In addition to the lying and stealing, Julie was beginning to engage in more sexualized behaviors with the other children in the home. This posed a very serious problem in the foster home, because all the other children were younger than Julie, with the exception of one child who was mentally impaired.

Julie was beginning to exhibit the same kinds of behaviors at school. She was being sent to the principal's office on a more regular basis. Her offenses at school included fighting with other children, disrespecting adults, defiance, and opposition.

Julie had not been sent to the principal's office due to any sexual behaviors; however, after she had been in treatment, she was able to admit there had been such situations. She had engaged in some "touching" and trying to coerce others into more sexual behaviors; she just had never been caught (for a discussion of children's abusive sexual behavior, see Chapter 1).

Julie was an extremely difficult youngster to work with because she had difficulties with forming attachments to others. Although she probably did not fit into the clinical category of being "unattached," she certainly experienced very unhealthy attachments, causing her to have disrupted attachments.

The following example was taken from a session held with Julie shortly before she was discharged to outpatient therapy. Although this was not the recommendation of the treatment team working with Julie, it was the decision made by the state mental health system.

Example of Activity #38

The session started with "Samantha's Story" being read to Julie. The following processing took place following the story.

Therapist Julie, what do you think the difference is between safe and unsafe secrets?

Julie Safe secrets are when you are happy, and unsafe secrets are when you are really unhappy.

T What do you think the safe or fun secret was in this story?

J The fun secret was Jamie's birthday party.

T Yeah, that was a secret that eventually she would know without anyone ever having to tell her. What do you think the unsafe or difficult secret in the story was?

J The bad secret was that she got touched where she wasn't supposed to be touched by her grandparent.

T Yeah, I don't think anyone is suppose to touch a kid there, do you? What do you think Samantha should do?

J   I think she should tell her parents what her grandpa is doing to
    her.
T   Yeah, I think you are right. Anytime someone is doing private
    touching with a kid, the kid should tell. I think it's really hard
    for some people to tell about it. I wish there was a way to make
    it easier for kids to talk about private touching stuff because a
    lot of times kids think it's their fault and it never is.
J   I don't even like talking about it.
T   Yeah, sometimes it's hard. What did you think about the story?
J   I didn't like the story because of the private touching.
T   Is private touching stuff kind of hard for you to talk about?
J   I just don't like it!
T   What is the difference between safe and unsafe or difficult
    secrets?
J   Safe is good, and difficult is bad.
T   Can you give me an example of a safe and unsafe secret.
J   A safe secret is when there is fun, like having a surprise party.
    And an unsafe secret is when you don't want to do something,
    or something bad happened.
T   How did you feel about Samantha's secret?
J   I felt bad because she should talk to someone about it.
T   It makes you want to help Samantha feel safe enough to talk
    about it, doesn't it? Have you ever had a secret that you thought
    you shouldn't tell or that was hard for you to tell?
J   NO!

Clinical Impressions: It is apparent that this girl is very resistant to
this activity. Most likely, it brought up difficult memories for her.
Her defense is to block the memories and deny any feelings associated with the unpleasant memories. Therefore, stories that approxi-
mate her life experiences may stimulate flashbacks. This could be
beneficial if the therapeutic rapport has been well established.

Julie appears very concrete in her approach to life. She redefines
safe as fun and unsafe as bad. This makes it easier for her to engage
in the activity. She has no concept of what being safe means; therefore, she replaces it with terms to which she can relate better.

The answers Julie gave to whether she liked the story and whether
she has ever had a secret that was hard to tell indicate just how

strong her denial is. It is clear from her history that she definitely had a difficult time telling her grandmother about her father's sexual abuse, yet she denies having this experience. Perhaps this is due to her grandmother's initial response, which was to believe her and seek assistance. Later, the grandmother withdrew her support and stated she didn't believe it ever happened. It is not uncommon for abused children to become very confused by others' responses to their disclosure. This is especially true if the initial response is to believe the child and then later renounce that belief. Many times, this experience leads children to repress or deny their abuse.

If this is how Julie has interpreted her previous experiences, ongoing trauma resolution work is going to be very difficult. She will most likely vacillate between Phases I and II for quite a while. As soon as she gets close to her trauma, she will probably withdraw emotionally for fear of rejection. This is the scenario played out with her grandmother. With patience and persistence, it is possible that Julie will eventually work through this difficult stage in her recovery.

❑ **Activity #39: Secrets Make Me Feel . . .**

Objective: To work on expressing feelings associated with secrets.

This activity is designed to allow children to express feelings associated with their secrets. Asking children to draw their feelings can be a less threatening technique, because breaking the code of secrecy can be such an overwhelming task for children. Drawing also can allow children to get more in touch with their subconscious feelings.

This activity may elicit a great deal of emotions, or you may find the child will shut down completely and deny any feelings or secrets. If the child is in denial, encourage him or her to draw a picture of how Samantha (from the previous activity) may have felt about her secrets. Or you can ask the child to pretend he or she had a secret and then draw a feelings picture.

Ages: This activity is designed for children of all ages as long as they can link up thoughts with feelings. The depth of the activity will correlate with the developmental age.

Materials Needed: Activity sheet and pencils, crayons, colored pencils, and/or markers.

Instructions: Instruct the child to think about his or her secrets and to be aware of any associated feelings. Then tell the child to draw a picture(s) of his or her feelings connected with the secrets.

Processing: After the child has finished the drawing, it is important to process the picture with him or her. We have found it helpful to ask, "Tell me about your picture. How do you feel about it?" "Is your secret(s) safe or unsafe? Why?" "Can you tell me about the secret(s) you thought about?"

It is also important to process with the child any feelings associated with sharing his or her secrets.

The following case example will illustrate how one physically and emotionally abused girl processed this activity.

Case Example: *Selina*

Brief Case History: Selina was a 6-year-old who was placed in the Partial Hospital Program due to her severe tantrums and rage episodes. This was the fifth removal for Selina by the state's Child Protective Services. Upon her admission to the Partial Hospital Program, Selina was living in a facility for children who were in the state's custody because they were not able to go to a foster home. In Selina's case, she was unable to be placed in a foster home due to her disruptive and aggressive behaviors.

Selina's previous removals from her mother's custody were due to neglect, abandonment, and physical abuse. She had been placed in the state's facility before on several occasions. This last removal was due to her grandfather's negligence. Her mother had left Selina and her older sister in his care while she was out on the streets using drugs and prostituting.

Selina's most recent removal occurred when she was discovered wandering down the middle of the road with her intoxicated grandfather. Selina and her sister were holding onto their grandfather's hands, one on each side. When the police officer discovered Selina and her sister, neither had eaten for a period of time.

The exact details of Selina's abuse history were not known upon her admission to the Partial Hospital Program. Throughout her treatment, Selina was able to work through some of her abuse history and share a few of her memories. It was clear that Selina had suffered physical abuse, including getting hit with shoes, belts, and other objects. In addition, she had been subject to emotional abuse, which included being belittled by her mother and her mother's boyfriends, being called names, and being cursed at by her caregivers.

It seemed the most damaging trauma Selina suffered was twofold. First, she witnessed a great deal of domestic violence between her mother and her mother's partners. She also witnessed a great deal of violence when she lived with her grandfather. Second, Selina was not nurtured by her mother or other caregivers. Selina did not learn how to trust others or allow others to soothe her when she was emotionally upset or hurt.

Although there was no known history of sexual abuse, Selina did show behaviors that were consistent with being exposed to sexually explicit materials and situations and/or being sexualized. She exposed herself to other children. She frequently violated the physical boundaries of others. She was indiscriminate with her affections toward others.

Throughout her treatment, Selina struggled with building therapeutic rapport and allowing herself to trust anyone. It was extremely difficult for Selina to share any personal information. This included things that occurred on a day-to-day basis, let alone her secrets from her past.

The following example was taken from a session toward the end of Selina's placement in the Partial Hospital Program. She had been returned to her mother's care following her mother's discharge from a drug and alcohol rehabilitation center. Selina and her mother continued to address her therapeutic issues in intensive outpatient therapy following her discharge from the Partial Hospital Program.

Example of Activity #39

The session began shortly after Selina was asked to come into the office. She initially looked around the room, which was typical of her, and then asked, "What are we going to do today?"

Therapist Well, Selina, I thought we could draw some pictures today.

Selina Pictures of what?

T   I thought maybe we could draw some pictures about how secrets make you feel.

S   I DON'T WANT TO TALK ABOUT MY SECRETS!

T   Wait a minute, Selina, I didn't say anything about you having to talk about secrets. I just said we were going to draw some pictures.

S: Oh, okay. As long as I don't have to talk about my secrets.

T   Now that we have that cleared up, why don't you come sit at the drawing table.

S   Okay. So what do I draw?

T   Well, I want you to think about your secrets. You know what secrets are, don't you?

S   Yep, secrets are about private stuff.

T   Are those the only things secrets are about?

S   Uh huh.

T   Okay, Selina, what I would like you to do is think for a minute about how secrets make you feel.

S   They make me feel sad, I don't want to talk about my secrets.

T   We already talked about this, you don't have to talk about anything if you don't want to. You can just draw a picture.

S   About how my secrets make me feel? I already said, "sad."

T   Can you draw a picture of your sad feelings?

S   A picture of myself?

T   Well it can be any kind of picture you want to draw about how secrets make you feel.

S   Okay, I'm going to draw myself. Should I draw my head first?

T   I think you should draw anything you want first. . . . It's your picture.

S   I'm going to draw my head. What color should I use? Any color I want?

T   It's your picture, you can use any color and draw it anyway you want.

Selina continued to draw the picture. She continued to ask questions about what color and what to draw, so the therapist said that they would talk once the picture was complete.

T   Selina, can you tell me about your picture?
S   This is me, and I feel sad.
T   And what do you feel sad about?
S   My secrets. But I don't want to talk about my secrets.
T   No one is saying you have to, but if you talked about your secrets maybe you wouldn't have to feel so sad.
S   No way!
T   What do you worry about most when you think about your secrets?
S   If I tell my secrets, other people will laugh at me.
T   Yeah, I've had lots of kids tell me that they worry about people laughing at them if they tell their secrets.
S   Not me.
T   But you know what, those same kids have told me that sharing their secrets makes them feel better.
S   But not me.
T   Well, if you ever want to talk about your secrets, Selina, I will listen and I promise I won't ever laugh at you.
S   I know.

The session ended soon after this discussion. Selina wanted to finish so that she could play.

Clinical Impressions: It is clear that this child needs to have control over every aspect of her environment. She attempts to control the direction of therapy, which works fine in this situation because she has been given control over the activity. However, at home and at school this could cause problems. She seems to find it difficult to trust caregivers and resists even the most minor suggestions.

It appears that Selina wants to share her secrets on some level but resists doing it if directed. When she states that she is fearful that other people would laugh at her secrets, the therapist assures her that other children have the same experience. This does not shake her resolve.

This need to control may stem from abuse-related anxiety, as suggested by Briere (1992). Briere relates Beck and Emery's cognitive model of anxiety disorder to abuse-related anxiety. He lists "hypervigilance to danger in the environment, preoccupation with control, and misinterpretation of objectively neutral or positive interpersonal stimuli as evidence of threat or danger" (p. 33).

Selina keeps herself emotionally disengaged throughout this activity. She uses every opportunity to resist getting into any feelings. Her self-portrait (see Illustration 6.1) is a regressed and immature picture depicting a sad-looking child. She includes no details. The picture looks vacant. It represents a fragmented sense of self. She indicated that the grass was at the bottom but she placed herself stranded in the sky, clearly not grounded.

At this stage in Selina's treatment, she needs to continue exploring her feelings and building trust with her therapist. In fact, it may be a good idea to go back to some earlier activities in the rapport-building phase and work on expressing feelings in general and building trust so that she will be able to explore her difficult and painful secrets. She does not seem ready to do this yet.

An interesting note to this case is that Selina had been able to explore her feelings and was beginning to engage in uncovering memories prior to her placement back with her mother. This session took place after she had gone back to live with her mother. It is clear that she has regressed in her ability to trust others.

❏ Activity #40: Safe Places to Share

Objective: To begin exploring safe places to share difficult secrets.

This activity is designed to introduce the child to appropriate and safe places to share difficult secrets. A discussion of appropriate and safe places should precede the activity because many abused children are confused by the concept of appropriateness.

Illustration 6.1.

Some children who have been abused may blurt out on the playground or in the middle of class that someone has touched their "privates." These children have no real concept of boundaries and, therefore, make statements at inappropriate times or places that can set them up to be shunned or ridiculed. Other children may be so rigid with boundaries that they retreat emotionally, never sharing thoughts or feelings with anyone.

Although each child is an individual and will react to stress in different ways, all abused children need to learn that there are safe places and times when they may share secrets. Therefore, your discussion with the child regarding safe and appropriate places to share difficult secrets is a necessary step in the recovery process.

Ages: This activity is designed for children ages 6 to 12.

Materials Needed: Activity sheet and crayons, colored pencils, and/or markers.

Instructions: Instruct the child to think about a place where he or she feels totally safe—a place where there is no physical or emotional pain. Then ask the child to draw a picture of this place. If the child can identify more than one safe place, encourage him or her to draw all of these places.

Note: Developmentally delayed or emotionally "stuck" children may draw very primitive pictures; however, their discussion of what it signifies is of prime importance. With these children, time must be taken to let them dictate what their picture is all about.

Processing: After the drawing is completed, it is important to process the picture with the child. We have found it helpful to ask, "Tell me about your picture(s)." "What makes you feel safe in this place(s)?" "Are there places where you don't feel safe? Tell me about them."

❑ Activity #41: I Can Tell!

Objective: To begin exploring who are appropriate and safe people to share secrets with.

This activity is designed to introduce the child to appropriate and safe people to share secrets with. A discussion of appropriate and safe people should precede this activity because many abused children are confused by the concept of appropriateness and which people in their environment are safe.

Many abused children are coerced to keep silent by their abusers. To add to their confusion, the abusers are often people they are supposed to trust. Thus, these children have difficulty discriminating between people who can and cannot be trusted.

Many times, abused children handle the above dilemma by refusing to talk at all or by talking incessantly to anyone and everyone they come in contact with. Therefore, your discussion with the child regarding safe and appropriate people to share difficult secrets with is a necessary step in the recovery process.

Ages: This activity is designed for children ages 6 to 12.

Materials Needed: Activity sheet and pencils, crayons, colored pencils, and/or markers.

Instructions: Instruct the child to think about the person or people with whom he or she feels totally safe. Many times, abused children do not feel totally safe with anyone. If this is the case, encourage the child to think about the person or people with whom he or she feels the safest.

Ask the child to write about or draw a picture of a person who has never hurt him or her and who can be trusted with difficult secrets. If the child can identify more than one person, encourage him or her to include all of these people.

Note: Even developmentally delayed children can draw stick figures or circles to indicate people in their life.

Processing: After the drawing is completed, it is important to process the picture with the child. We have found it helpful to ask, "Tell me about the person or people." "What makes you feel safe with this person or with these people?" "Are there any people with whom you don't feel safe? Tell me about them."

❏ Activity #42: My Friend's Secret

Objective: To explore difficult secrets through the medium of writing stories.

This activity is designed to use the storytelling technique to encourage children to explore their difficult secrets. Often, it is easier for children to process their own secrets by projecting their experiences as "a friend's" secret. Asking children to make up a story about another child allows them to expose their own secrets while pretending they are someone else's. This frees them up to explore feelings associated with difficult or painful secrets, because they don't feel as threatened when attributing feelings to others.

Ages: This activity is primarily designed for children who are functioning at an independent level and are able to write sentences on their own. However, it can be modified to work with lower-functioning children by simply having them dictate the story to you.

Materials Needed: Activity sheet and pencils.

Instructions: Instruct the child to think of a story about a child who has a difficult secret. Encourage the child to talk about the story before either writing or dictating. Once the child has created the story, instruct him or her to write or dictate the story he or she related.

Processing: After the child has finished writing the story, it is important to discuss the child's impressions of the story and how it related to him or her. We have found it also helpful to ask, "Tell me about your story." "How do you think the person in your story feels about his or her secret?" "Did the kid find someone safe to talk to? Why? Who?" "Are you like the kid in your story? How?"

Case Example: *Janie*

Brief Case History: Janie was a 9-year-old who was placed in the Partial Hospital Program following her discharge from an acute hospitalization unit in a psychiatric facility. Janie was hospitalized due to her self-injurious behaviors (biting herself, making suicidal threats, and pulling out her toenails) and "hearing voices."

Janie's subsequent placement in the Partial Hospital Program, following her hospitalization, was to help support her in a less restrictive environment while still addressing her therapeutic needs. Janie continued to have multiple behavioral difficulties following her hospitalization, including encopresis, enuresis, frequent mood swings, defiance, and oppositional behavior.

When Janie was initially admitted to the Partial Hospital Program, she was in her third year as a ward of the state. She had been removed from her biological mother's care following numerous reports of neglect and a final report of physical abuse. It was reported that Janie's mother hit her with a belt across her back and left welts.

Janie also reported allegations of sexual abuse once she was in the state's care. Reportedly, a couple of Janie's paternal uncles molested her when she went to visit her father in another state.

Janie had been placed in several foster homes and the state's facility for children throughout her 3 years. She continually was disrupted from placements due to her out-of-control and aggressive behaviors. Throughout Janie's placements, she had been treated with various kinds of medication in an attempt to help her control her behavior. It seemed the pharmacological approach alone did not meet Janie's needs, because she continued to experience a great deal of distress.

When Janie was admitted to the Partial Hospital Program, she presented much differently than her history had indicated. She typically would isolate herself from other children. This did not seem to be due to her shyness or fear but rather from a position that she was better or more special than the other children.

She also was very demanding and would throw a tantrum at any time when she did not get her own way. It seemed from a strictly behavioral stance that Janie was a very overindulged child. This, however, could not have been further from the truth, because she spent her first 6 years in a near-poverty-stricken family.

Janie also was practically oblivious to other people's boundaries. This was primarily directed toward adults, because she typically kept herself away from other children. Janie frequently would run up and give adults hugs. She would plop herself on someone's lap without first asking permission. In addition, when she was sitting on an adult's lap, she would begin caressing arms, legs, backs, shoulders, and at times would seemingly attempt to touch in the chest area.

In Janie's first 6 years with her biological family, she was exposed to a great deal of domestic violence between her mother and father. Her needs frequently were ignored because both of her parents drank heavily and were using crack cocaine. When Janie was approximately 4 years old, her mother and father were divorced. Her father moved to another state, and Janie's older brother moved with him. Janie's mother was involved with several men over a very short period of time until she met her third husband, Janie's stepfather.

Although the arguing continued with Janie's mother and stepfather, the physical fighting had stopped. This was the "best" environment of Janie's short 6 years. However, Janie's mother continued to parent the way in which her abusive mother had parented her. This is when Janie was removed due to the physical abuse.

The focus of Janie's treatment in the Partial Hospital Program was trauma resolution. The hope was that Janie could get her own behaviors under enough control that a fair determination of return to parent could be reached. Janie's parents, mother and stepfather, continued to participate in therapy and drug rehabilitation. They had made so much progress that the state's social worker was recommending return to parent.

The following example is taken from a session with Janie several months into her treatment. Change with Janie was extremely slow because she continued to "roller-coaster" with her ability to control her own behaviors. Thus, much time was spent on simply assisting her own developing internal controls of her behaviors in order to continue working on trauma issues.

Eventually it was determined that simply being away from her mother was producing a great deal of stress for Janie. Visitation was once again established with Janie and her mother and stepfather. Shortly thereafter, the visits turned into "therapeutic" visits. This allowed Janie to begin settling down behaviorally and focusing on trauma resolution work.

Example of Activity #42

The following example was taken from an individual session held following Janie's return to her family. Janie was instructed to think about a kid who had a difficult secret. She was then instructed to make up a story about this child. Once she was ready to dictate her story, she was told that the therapist would be a "secretary" for her.

Therapist Do you know how you want your story to go?

Janie Yeah. Once upon a time there was a little girl.

T Does she have a name?

J Yes, it's Janie. It's a story about me.

T It's your story, so it can be about anybody you want. What do you want to write next?

J She had a hard time talking about her secret. Janie didn't tell her mom and dad what happened with her uncle because she was too scared.

T What was she scared about?

J She was scared to tell because she thought she might get in trouble. She thought her mom and dad would yell at her.

T Why did she think they would yell at her?

J I don't know!

T Oh, okay, so what happened?

J After thinking for a long time Janie decided to tell her mom and dad, at a meeting in her house, about her uncle.

T And what happened?

J Her mom and dad didn't yell.

T What did they do?

J I don't know. But after she told her secret she felt very happy.

T Then what happened?

J Janie learned that telling her mom and dad hard secrets was good.

T That's a great story, Janie—let me read the whole thing to you. Then if you want to add anything or change anything you can.

J Okay.

The story was then read. Janie decided that she liked it just the way it was.

Clinical Impressions: It seems that Janie was therapeutically ready to approach this activity. She seemed comfortable with dictating her story and revealing her own issues rather than making up a story about someone else. This indicates that she has completed Phase I of her recovery process.

Janie seems to have a healthy, therapeutic relationship. She does not seem overly involved or resistant to questions by the therapist.

She was able to provide an optimistic resolution to her story, which was consistent with life events.

This child has been damaged by her abuse but has retained enough sense of self to allow her to share her sexual abuse with her mother and stepfather. Janie has a history of physical abuse by her mother and has seemingly resolved any sense of betrayal by her mother. Janie may be ready to move to the next phase of recovery due to her extensive history of therapeutic intervention.

❏ Activity #43: My Happy Secret

Objective: To learn about safe and unsafe secrets.

This activity is designed to encourage the child to begin exploring the differences between safe and unsafe secrets. Children who have been abused often lump all secrets together, assuming that they should not divulge any secrets at all. These children need to learn how to differentiate between different kinds of secrets and learn that it is okay to reveal secrets that are harmful.

Because young children are so concrete and "black and white" in their thinking, it is easier to begin with differentiating between safe and unsafe secrets. Once children are able to make this distinction, they will be better equipped to sort out the secrets that should be shared. With this skill, children will be able to protect themselves more easily in future situations.

Ages: This activity is designed for children of all ages.

Materials Needed: Activity sheet and pencils, crayons, colored pencils, and/or markers.

Instructions: Instruct the child to think back to a time when someone told them a fun secret. Then ask the child to write or draw about a time when he or she told someone a fun or safe secret.

Note: The higher-functioning child may want to write and draw a picture, but the lower-functioning child may only be able to draw a picture with assistance.

Processing: After the child has completed the activity, it is important to discuss the activity with him or her. We have found it helpful to ask, "Tell me about your fun secret." "Who did you tell your fun secret to? Why?" "How did you feel when you told your secret?" "How do you think your friend felt when you told your secret?"

❏ **Activity #44: My Difficult Secret**

Objective: To continue learning about safe and unsafe secrets but focusing this time on unhappy or difficult secrets.

This activity is designed to encourage the child to continue the process of differentiating between safe and unsafe secrets. This will probably be a more difficult task for the child, because this activity focuses on unpleasant memories.

It is important for you, as the child's therapist, to be extremely sensitive to the difficulty of this process. It may provoke a variety of feelings in the child, which can become somewhat overwhelming. Again, so often abused children use defiance as a coping mechanism to avoid confronting these overwhelming feelings.

When children become defiant and resistant in therapy, it may provoke countertransference issues. You may find yourself reacting with anger. It is important to recognize your own feelings so that you do not allow this to interfere with the therapeutic process. Children need lots of empathy, encouragement, and support during this potentially difficult time.

Ages: This activity is designed for children of all ages.

Materials Needed: Activity sheet and pencils, crayons, colored pencils, and/or markers.

Instructions: Instruct the child to think about a time when someone shared a difficult or scary secret. Then ask the child to write or draw a picture of a time when he or she told someone a difficult secret. If the child has never shared a difficult or scary secret, ask him or her to write or draw about what it might be like to share.

Note: The higher-functioning child may choose to write and draw a picture about sharing difficult secrets. The lower-functioning child may only be able to draw a picture with assistance.

Processing: After the child has completed the activity, it is important to discuss and process the difficult secret. We have found it helpful to ask, "Tell me about your difficult or scary secret." "Who did you tell your secret to?" "Why did you pick this person?" "How did you feel when you told your secret?" "How do you think your friend felt when you shared your secret? Why?"

7

Memories, Nightmares, and "Monsters"

For many child victims of abuse, remembering may be the first step toward healing. This may be the most difficult step for children, because many abusive experiences happen at the preverbal or beginning stages of language acquisition. These children had no way of verbalizing, understanding, or making sense of what was happening to them.

Children who are traumatized prior to their ability to form narrative memories often play out these memories, and they often fear trauma-related stimuli (Terr, 1994). This can be seen in the play of abused children.

Children are born with basic instincts and needs, such as sucking, touching, and being held. They are unable to distinguish between "appropriate" and "inappropriate" behaviors. Therefore, when others victimize them, they are unable to label the behavior as abusive.

Obviously, this makes it difficult to help children uncover and work through their experiences.

In addition to the difficulty of working through preverbal experiences, some children may "block" or repress memories. Repression or dissociation is a coping mechanism that occurs when an individual unconsciously avoids anxiety and distress associated with painful memories (Briere, 1992; Briere & Conte, 1993).

Whereas the capacity for storage of memory is almost limitless, the retrieval can be difficult, especially if the memory is painful. Due to the nature of memory retrieval, many researchers have suggested that children's memories are "suggestible," but others have found children's memories to be quite resilient (Doris, 1991). This has set forth the notion of a false memory syndrome (no such proven syndrome) as an explanation for recovered memories. This debate has created quite a controversy within the mental health field (Karp, 1995).

Terr (1994) stresses the notion that conflict is the key to repression. There is an unwillingness or inability for trauma victims to accept that someone they trusted has abused them. Gil (1991) describes dissociation as "a process of separating, segregating, and isolating chunks of information, perceptions, memories, motivations, and affects" (p. 22).

There also may be a feeling of danger associated with exposing the perpetrator(s). Some children still may be living with or near the perpetrator(s). Other children may have been "threatened" if they reveal the abuse. Thus, these children may consciously deny, block, or suppress the memory as a survival mechanism.

Dreams can be one vehicle to help children uncover repressed or blocked memories. As Gil (1991) points out, it is believed that dreams are an individual's way of allowing unresolved traumas to leak into consciousness. Dreams also may allow the individual to rehearse things to come. Therefore, it is a useful technique to have children share their dreams and nightmares as a nonthreatening or nondirective means of working through abusive memories.

It is important to keep in mind that dreams and nightmares can be somewhat distorted aspects of reality. However, over time, bits of the dreams will fit together, much like pieces of a puzzle will, helping the child to remember abusive experiences.

When children draw or relate characters in their dreams or fears, they often talk about "monsters." Therefore, it is important to have children confront their "monsters." In doing so, this can give the child a sense of empowerment and control over their fears, allowing them to work through their memories.

There are several goals for this chapter. First, it is important to remember that working through abuse is a long-term process. This chapter, as all previous chapters, is the beginning point of retrieving and working through memories. There is no right or wrong way to do this.

One goal is to assist children in the process of remembering their abuse. Terr (1994) points out that dreams are important to trauma but are not always connected to trauma. Children do not necessarily dream about their particular trauma. However, some people who repress do dream, particularly as their memories begin to come back toward the surface. Repeated dreams seem, in particular, to be connected to terrifying experiences derived from actual outside events (Terr, 1990).

Another goal is to assist children in confronting their "monsters," which addresses an underlying therapeutic goal of developing a sense of empowerment. Again, it is important to help children realize that they have control over their perceived "monsters," because they are battling fears, not the actual perpetrators.

The activities in this chapter are designed to assist children in their ability to process and problem solve the memories, nightmares, and "monsters" so common to many abused children. As the child begins to "unlock" the secrets associated with the abuse, memories will begin to emerge. These memories may surface in many forms. The child may experience nightmares, recurring dreams, or flashbacks. This may be a particularly difficult and frightening period in the child's treatment.

This is a very painful point in the child's recovery process and it can, therefore, be an intense experience for the therapist, both personally and professionally. It is important for you, as the child's therapist, to remember that the goal is to help guide the child through his or her thoughts and feelings so that the child gains a sense of empowerment. This sense of personal control over his or her "monsters" leads to a healthier sense of self.

One method of gaining mastery over the child's fears is to use a technique discussed by Mills and Crowley in *Therapeutic Metaphors for Children and the Child Within* (1986) and *Cartoon Magic* (1989). They suggest having the child identify a favorite cartoon friend who can help him or her with the monster. They also suggest including the parents in this process by having the parents provide paper and markers near the child's bed so that when the child wakes in the middle of the night scared, he or she can continue the process started in therapy.

Because this can be such an intense or emotionally charged experience, you may find it necessary to consult with a colleague to work through your own countertransference issues (Gil & Johnson, 1993). This is a time when you may be getting many phone calls from caretakers, teachers, and other concerned adults regarding the child's behavior and their concerns of how to assist the child. Although this is a difficult time for the therapist and child, it is necessary and can be a pivotal point in the child's recovery.

The following activities are designed to assist children in exploring and working through difficult and painful memories, scary nightmares, or bad dreams and to confront their "monsters."

A few case studies have been included to assist you in further understanding of how some of these activities have been used in actual therapy situations. We have provided a brief case history, an example of dialogue between the therapist and child during the activity, and clinical impressions of the child's work.

As we have stated in previous chapters, the Activity Book includes a "Message to the Kids" section. You may want to give the child a copy of the one for this chapter. It provides the child with a brief introduction to the concepts covered in this chapter. It then can be placed in the child's folder or notebook with the other materials completed thus far. It is a good idea to go over this with the child before beginning the activities in this chapter.

❑ **Activity #45: I Had a Dream**

Objective: To begin looking at and processing dreams.

This activity is designed to introduce the child to the concept of exploring dreams. This first activity is set up so that there is no expectation of what kind of dream may be explored. The idea is to just introduce the child to drawing about dreams—whether the dreams are happy, sad, scary, and so on.

As stated previously, dreams can be a nondirective vehicle to explore unresolved trauma. However, before unresolved trauma can be addressed, children may need to learn and practice how to simply draw and describe a dream of their choice. This could be a scary dream, but it also may be a dream of a funny movie or a delightful experience they had.

Ages: This activity is designed for children ages 6 to 12.

Materials Needed: Activity sheet and crayons, markers, and/or colored pencils.

Instructions: Instruct the child to draw a picture of a dream he or she has had. Discuss all kinds of dreams with the child, including dreams of movies and so on, to help stimulate thinking about dreams he or she has had. It is hoped that the discussion will allow the child to explore a variety of dreams freely.

Note: The younger child may draw stick figures and have little content, but the older child may have lots of details.

Processing: After the child has completed the drawing, it is important to discuss it by asking, "Tell me about your dream." "How does this dream make you feel? Why?" "How did you feel while you were drawing your dream?" "Why did you pick this dream to draw?"

❑ Activity #46: My Happy Dream

Objective: To process feelings associated with a pleasant dream.

This activity is designed to explore feelings associated with dreams. It is usually less threatening to begin this process by connecting "happy" feelings with dreams.

As hard as some therapists try to direct children to explore positive feelings, some children will perseverate on the negative. Some children may in fact try to gain a sense of power by expressing pleasure when they have been the aggressor in a scary dream, thereby trying to say that this was a happy dream. This needs to be explored with the child. It is clear that the child is confused about the feelings associated with aggression, in that the "happy" feeling is associated with violence, power, and control over another individual.

It will be important to process with the child what the child will be drawing prior to the activity so the above concerns can be addressed, if necessary. Also, it will be important to process feelings as the child draws the picture of the dream.

Ages: This activity is designed for children ages 6 to 12 as long as they can identify feelings associated with dreams.

Materials Needed: Activity sheet and crayons, colored pencils, and/or markers.

Instructions: Instruct the child to draw a picture of a dream that made him or her feel happy. As stated above, if the child is at a concrete level of development, it may be necessary to restructure this activity to just focus on feelings.

Note: If the child is very concrete, it may be necessary to restructure this activity and direct the child to draw a picture of what makes the child "happy," excluding the concept of feelings associated with dreams.

Processing: After the child has drawn his or her picture, it is important to follow up with questions such as "Tell me about your happy dream." "What makes this a happy dream? " "Have you had other dreams that made you feel happy? Tell me about them."

□ **Activity #47: My Scary Dream**

Objective: To process feelings associated with scary dreams.

This activity is designed to help the child explore dreams that have frightened the child. With the advent of movies, television, and other products of mass media, children have been exposed to stimuli that may result in bad dreams. In addition, children have been exposed to storybooks that talk all about children's experiences with bad dreams, monsters (in their closets), nightmares, and so on. Therefore, this activity most likely will be familiar to the child and something the child will probably want to do.

Ages: This activity is designed for children ages 6 to 12 as long as they are able to connect feelings with dreams.

Materials Needed: Activity sheet and crayons, colored pencils, and/or markers.

Instructions: Instruct the child to draw a picture of a dream that made him or her feel scared. Again, if the child is functioning at a very concrete level, instruct him or her to focus on something that creates scary feelings rather than drawing a picture of a dream.

Note: Even preschoolers are exposed to picture books about scary dreams; however, at that age, they rarely connect their own feelings with dreams. It is important to assess whether the child has the capacity to connect feelings with dreams.

As in the previous activity, it may be necessary to modify this activity to simply explore scary feelings rather than scary feelings associated with dreams.

Processing: After the child has completed drawing his or her scary dream, it is important to discuss the dream with questions such as "Tell me about your scary dream." "What makes this dream scary to you?" "Have you had other dreams that are frightening? Tell me about them."

❏ Activity #48: The Never-Ending Dream

Objective: To explore dreams that are recurring.

This activity is designed to encourage the child to explore dreams that are recurring. Recurring dreams can be extremely valuable in terms of the child's treatment. As previously stated, dreams can be the roadway into unresolved trauma. Thus, recurring dreams tend to be significant in that they may serve as a "red flag" that the child is attempting to resolve some internal conflict.

Recurring dreams also can serve another important function in the child's therapy. They can be used as yardsticks to measure progress in terms of internal resolution. You may find that over time the child's recurring dream changes. It is important to monitor the changes, focusing on mastery and empowerment.

This activity is designed for children who have had recurring dreams. It can be very powerful for these children. Obviously, if a child has not experienced a recurring dream, this activity may be skipped.

Ages: Children ages 6 to 12 should be able to participate in this activity as long as they are able to understand the concept of recurring dreams.

Materials Needed: Activity sheet and crayons, colored pencils, and/or markers.

Instructions: Instruct the child to think about a dream that he or she has had more than one time. Then tell the child to draw a picture of this dream. It will be important to process the feelings associated with the child's recurring dream while he or she is drawing.

Note: In order for this activity to be successful, the child must be able to connect feelings with dreams. Developmentally delayed children may have difficulty with this concept.

Processing: After the child is finished with this activity, it is important to discuss the picture by asking, "Tell me about the dream you keep having." "How does this dream make you feel?" "How did it feel to draw this picture?" "How would you like to change your dream?"

The following case example will illustrate how one sexually, physically, and emotionally abused child processed this activity.

Case Example: *Kenya*

Brief Case History: Kenya was a 10-year-old who was referred to the Partial Hospital Program by her adoption caseworker. She was placed in a foster-adopt family, with the possibility of an adoption depending on her ability to "fit" into the family and decrease her problematic behaviors.

When Kenya was initially placed in the Partial Hospital Program, she demonstrated a multitude of behaviors that left people wondering if she had psychotic features. She frequently got on the floor of her classroom and barked like a dog. In addition, she would crawl under desks, refusing to come out. She also would be physically assaultive to children and adults when she got overly stressed.

Kenya also would engage in many sexual behaviors that included exposing herself to others, masturbating in the classroom, taking off her clothing in the school bathroom, and attempting to touch other children's genitals. Kenya's sexual behaviors had gotten to such an extreme that her foster-adopt mother would allow her only to wear jeans and shorts, rather than a dress, to school as a means to deter her from exposing herself.

Kenya was the youngest of three children. She and her brothers were born to a heroin-addicted mother who used during all of her pregnancies. Kenya had been removed from her mother's care several times before the age of 3. Her mother always was able to do the bare minimum required to have the children returned to her.

The state took final custody of Kenya when they found out that she and her brothers had been stealing from a convenience store, which was located almost one and a half miles from their apartment. Kenya was dressed in only her diapers. The children were then placed in a foster home.

In the foster home, Kenya and her brothers were subject to severe physical, emotional, and sexual abuse as well as neglect. The children remained in the home for several years, as it was located in a rural area and social workers did not visit often. Eventually, the foster home was shut down. Kenya and her brothers were removed from the home before it was closed and were placed in the foster-adopt home.

Therapy with Kenya was long-term, given her extensive abuse history and severe behavioral difficulties. It took several months for Kenya to work through Phase I, building therapeutic rapport, because her previous life experiences led her to develop such a view of the world that she would not feel safe. Thus, developing trust with anyone else was extremely difficult for her.

The following example was taken from a session held with Kenya in which she was working through a recurring dream. Kenya had a history of significant difficulties at bedtime. She eventually needed medication to assist her with sleep.

Example of Activity #48

Prior to working on Kenya's recurring dream, the first 15 minutes of the session were spent playing with dolls. This was somewhat of a ritual for Kenya. At the beginning of each session, she would feed and rock the dolls; she then would return them to their cribs and the session would continue.

Therapist Are you ready to work on that dream you keep having?
Kenya Yes, but what are we going to do?

T   Well, I was thinking that you could draw a picture of it, that way I can understand it a little bit better.

K   Okay. This is a dream I have had lots of times and it is really scary. (She proceeded to draw the picture, Illustration 7.1.)

T   Can you tell me about your dream?

K   I am in my bedroom. My mom was in my room and then she got kidnapped by a man. I tried to save my mom but the man pushed me away from my mom.

T   Can you remember anything else from your dream?

K   No.

T   I want you to think for a minute, I want you to think about how you could change your dream so that you would not feel so afraid at night. You will need to have your dream start out the same and then you can change it anyway you want to.

K   My mom was in my room and then a man came in my room and tried to kidnap both of us. Me and my mom tried to get away from him. I pulled my hand away from him and called 911. The police came over to my house and took him to jail. And then me and my mom were safe.

The rest of the session was spent discussing how Kenya could rework frightening dreams so that they are not so overwhelming.

Clinical Impressions: Kenya's history of recurring dreams really fits well for this activity. She also was very motivated to change the dream. It is important to note that her drawing is fanciful in many respects. She draws a picture of herself (see Illustration 7.1) in bed with a heart above her, which includes her and her mother. Then she goes on to describe this terrible dream of someone kidnapping her mother.

This activity reflects Kenya's need to be in a "caretaking" role, as she does with her dolls. Her dream of not being able to protect her mother reflects how she was never taken care of by her biological mother. Even her change in the dream is of her calling 911, not her mother.

Because Kenya never is "taken care of" in her scenarios, one would suspect that she may suffer from an attachment disorder to some degree. This is reflected in her individual therapy sessions. She seems to jump into things with little emotion. There is some indica-

Illustration 7.1.

tion that at least she is conflicted over this lack of protection and wants it to change. She did form a positive therapeutic bond with her therapist but demonstrated severe damage to her sense of self.

Further sessions need to address her own needs rather than her continuing to be the "caretaker." She has made some movement, but due to the difficulty in her current situation (disruption in adoption), she will need long-term therapy if a positive resolution to her trauma is to occur. Because the adoption ended up falling through in some respects (adoptive mother and father divorced), further work on the ability to trust will be needed. Unless traumatized children have a fairly solid base, their ability to work through trauma-specific issues is limited.

❏ **Activity #49: My Monster**

Objective: To begin looking at various "monsters" that are found in dreams and other places.

This activity is designed to allow the child to begin to confront any "monsters" they may fear. Often, children who have been abused talk about "monsters." Initially, they may not connect these "monsters" with their abuse history. However, as they progress in therapy, these children often begin to talk about the "monster" who hurt them as they become empowered to face their abuse.

In her art therapy book, *Breaking the Silence: Art Therapy With Children From Violent Homes,* Malchiodi (1990) describes a commonality in artwork among children of battered women. The metaphor depicted in their drawings was of a monster of some sort. Other times, the monster was not as clear but equally powerful.

> These are the invisible monsters that gnaw away at the inner self, creatures that destroy self-esteem and leave in their wake anxiety and pain. For children from violent homes, the monsters can be an abusive parent, neglect, incest, and severe emotional trauma. (p. 4)

Children may approach this activity from many different perspectives according where they are individually and emotionally in their own recovery program. If children are rather disconnected from their feelings, this may prove to be a "fun" activity, with very little evidence of stress. However, if children are at all connected to the trauma of the abuse, they may experience a tremendous amount of stress and anxiety while engaging in this activity. As the child's therapist, it is important for you to attend to the child's reaction as he or she embarks on this activity.

Ages: This activity is designed for children of all ages.

Materials Needed: Activity sheet and pencils, crayons, colored pencils, and/or markers.

Instructions: Instruct the child to draw a picture of his or her "monster." A discussion about monsters that either the child has talked about or monsters that are in stories should precede the instruction. You may want to read Mayer's picture books *There's a Nightmare in My Closet* (1986) and *There's Something in My Attic* (1988).

Note: It is more important to focus on the child's level of emotional functioning rather than the chronological age.

Processing: After the child has completed his or her drawing, it is important to follow up with questions such as "Tell me about your monster." "How did you feel when you drew your monster?" "Tell me about your feelings."

The following case example will illustrate how one abused child processed this activity.

Case Example: *Mark*

Brief Case History: Mark was a 6-year-old who was admitted to a 3-hour Partial Hospital Program when he was beginning to show signs of regression in his adopted home and in his school placement. Mark was adopted when he was approximately 3 years old. He had been with this family since he was 2 years old.

Mark was given up for adoption by his mother at the time of his birth. His biological mother was addicted to drugs and did not feel able to meet Mark's needs. For some unknown reason, Mark was put in a foster home instead of being placed in a foster-adopt home or an adoptive home as an infant. It was in his first placement that Mark suffered the majority of his abuse.

It seems Mark's first foster mother was not nurturing and did not assist him in developing a healthy bond and/or attachment. Mark was left in his crib for long periods of time without being held or having any interactions. She apparently left bottles propped up in his crib in order to feed him. Mark was in this home until he needed to be hospitalized for failure to thrive at the age of 7 months. He was in the hospital for almost 3 months before he was well enough to be discharged.

When Mark was released from the hospital, he was placed in another foster home. Although it seems he was not purposely abused in this home, he ended up being removed due to breaking his femur in a "Johnnie Jumper." Apparently, his foster mother put Mark in the "long" Johnnie Jumper seat and hooked him into the short doorway, resulting in him hitting the floor and breaking his leg.

Following this incident, Mark was placed with his now adoptive parents. They were involved in a great deal of therapy, including bonding and attachment therapy with him. He also attended a thera-peutic preschool program prior to being enrolled in the first grade in the public school system. Shortly after his placement in school, Mark began to show signs of regression, including self-abusive behaviors, nightmares, lying and stealing, increased opposition and defiance with all authority figures, and isolation from his peers.

The following examples come from the work that Mark did in Phase II of his recovery process. Due to the early neglect, Mark was unable to form the appropriate and healthy attachments that all children need to grow up with a solid foundation. Mark spent a great deal of time working on issues in this phase, because develop-ing a sense of trust was extremely difficult for him. Because Mark was abused before he was verbal, it was extremely difficult for him to pinpoint exactly where his fears came from. Thus, Mark had many fears and frequently had difficulty sleeping, had frequent night-mares, and often talked about "monsters" coming to get him.

Example of Activity #49

Therapist   How are you doing today, Mark? Mom tells me you have had some trouble going to sleep lately. Are you thinking about something before you fall asleep, or are you worried about something?

Mark   Yes, I'm worried that the monsters are going to come and get me.

T   Those monsters can be pretty scary, and I know we've talked about them before. Remember, we talked about the monsters as things that you make in your own mind?

M   Yeah.

T   If you can make the monsters, you can make the monsters go away, too. I wonder if you can draw a picture of your monsters, and then we can figure out some ways for you to keep your monsters away at night.

M I can draw them, but can I draw each one on a different piece of paper?

T Sure, Mark, you can draw your monsters any way you want. Remember, they are your monsters, so you can do whatever you want with them.

M This is a scary pink monster. He has a fat body with a long, sharp tail. He has long nails and big feet that go hump, hump, hump.

T Do you want me to write down your words so that we can remember which monster was which?

M That's okay. Can you write the words right here?

T Sure I can. You want me to write that this is a scary pink monster. He has a fat body with a long, sharp tail. He has long nails and big feet that go hump, hump, hump. Is that right?

M Yeah that's right. Sometimes this monster scares me at night, so I shut my closet and I shut my curtains so the monster won't come inside my bedroom.

T Wow. It sounds like you are really scared at night. Do you know why the monster would want to come and get you?

M No. I just know that I really feel scared, and it makes it hard for me to fall asleep.

T I bet it's hard to fall asleep when you feel so scared. It sounds like you are already doing something, like closing your closet and shutting your curtains, to take care of yourself. I wonder if you can do anything else or get help from anyone else in your house?

M I don't know.

T Well is there anyone in your house that you can trust to keep you safe from getting hurt or help you when you are feeling scared?

M I think my mom and dad.

T Well, have you told them about the scary monsters and asked them to help you?

M No, but I probably can.

T I think that would be a good idea. How do you think you could ask them?

The rest of this session was spent doing role-playing to help Mark feel more confident about asking his mom and dad for help. The next dialogue is from the next session held with Mark. Notice the change in his wording regarding his "monster" and the difference in his confidence in his parents' support.

M This is a big, huge, orange monster. He was spanking me when I was littler. He was mad.

T Do you know why the monster was mad, Mark?

M No, I just know that he was mad. I guess he was mad at me for something, but I don't know why.

T Okay. Do you want me to write your words on your picture so that we don't forget which monster is which?

M Yep, and I want you to write, "It's not okay for the monster to hit me, so now I live at my mommy and daddy's house."

T So you know that when you are at your mommy and daddy's house, you are safe. The big, huge, orange monster cannot get you there, huh? That must make you feel happy knowing that your mom and dad are going to keep you safe from scary things. It's good that you can trust them.

M Yeah, I want you to write that, too.

T What do you want me to write?

M "The monster can't get me anymore because my mom and dad is here."

T Okay, Mark, I can do that. Is that all you wanted to say about this monster?

M Yep. I don't have to be scared about the monsters anymore because I know my mommy and daddy won't let anything happen to me. They told me it was their job to make sure I'm safe; and if I ever get scared, I can go get one of them.

The rest of this session was spent doing role-playing to assist Mark in going to his mom or dad to ask for help during different times of the day and night.

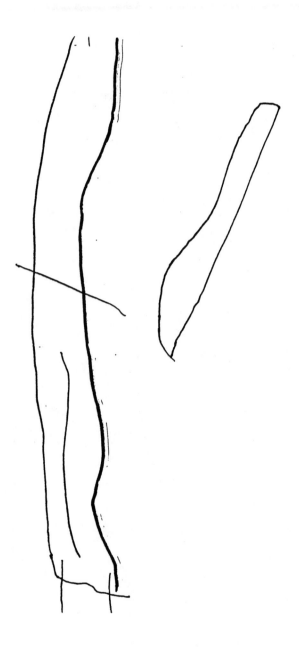

Illustration 7.2.

Illustration 7.3.

Clinical Impressions: The pictures (illustrations 7.2 and 7.3) reveal a rather immature and regressive portrayal of the monsters described in therapy. Analytically speaking, the monsters appear to be a phallic symbol. However, there is no known history of sexual abuse. Instead, the pictures seem to be at the level of a 3-year-old. This is an important note since it would be easy to become distracted by Mark's drawings and assume that they depict the monsters as "penises" coming after him. His history and therapy do not support this interpretation.

It is important not to jump to conclusions or interpretations from one drawing. Mark was a severely neglected child who was very regressed in his development. He suffered from failure to thrive and was an unbonded and unattached child.

There is a positive movement from the first to the second session. In the first session, Mark seemed isolated within his family, seeing no one as keeping him safe. This is understandable because he was so neglected in his various foster homes. Those who were supposed to keep him safe and loved completely ignored his needs. At the end of the first session, he did begin exploring who he could go to for help. This was followed by role-playing.

In the second session, he seemed much more confident that his mom and dad could keep him safe. There was a greater sense that he had embraced the notion that they really would keep him safe, that it was their "job." It appears that Mark was able to use the skills from his first session to build on in his next session.

It is important to note that Mark has had a great deal of therapy and still needs more. He had progressed fairly well until he entered first grade. The change from a half-day program to a full-day program was just too much for him to handle. He regressed quite a bit at that point. This is reflected in his current fears, which have resurfaced in the form of "monsters."

This is not an uncommon scenario. It isn't unusual to see traumatized preschool children reenter therapy at different points in their development as they are faced with new challenges and stressors. This shouldn't be looked at as a "failure" of previous therapeutic interventions. Rather, it is a continuation of the child's emerging sense of self.

❏ **Activity #50: Cartoon Helper**

Objective: To explore fears through the process of cartoon helpers.

This activity is designed to begin the problem-solving and empowerment process. After the child has identified his or her monster, the next step is to begin mastering the fears associated with it. As stated earlier, using cartoon friends can be a powerful technique in helping to resolve fear associated with trauma (Crowley & Mills, 1989).

Children love cartoons. This can be an excellent medium in which to engage children because they are able to enter their own imaginary world. Cartoons allow children to have fun and find humor while providing powerful symbolism. Thus, cartoons become metaphoric symbols, allowing children to "walk through the trauma" and gain a sense of empowerment.

We realize that this activity alone will not solve the child's problems or resolve the trauma. It will begin the process of mastery over difficult experiences.

This activity is structured so that the child can identify a cartoon helper that can help in dealing with the "monster" identified in Activity #49.

Ages: Children ages 6 to 12 should have no problem identifying a cartoon character that symbolizes "the hero" that can help solve problems.

Materials Needed: Activity sheet and pencils, crayons, colored pencils, and/or markers.

Instructions: Instruct the child to draw a picture of a cartoon character that he or she identifies as a special helper. Then direct the child to begin exploring the possibility of this special helper assisting in dealing with the monster (as identified in the previous activity).

Note: The developmental level of the child will dictate just how much processing can be accomplished with this activity. Not only can the child draw a picture of his or her special helper, but he or she actually can create cartoon strips to assist creating positive solutions to problems the child may have faced or is facing.

Processing: After the child has drawn a cartoon helper, it would be helpful to follow up with questions such as "Tell me about your cartoon helper." "What can your special helper do to help you with your monster?" "How does it feel to have a special helper? Why?"

The following case example will illustrate how one abused child processed this activity.

Case Example: *Sergio*

Brief Case History: Sergio was 9 years old when he was referred to the Partial Hospital Program by the state mental health system and his local school district. Sergio previously had received approximately 2 years of outpatient therapy; however, his behaviors seemed to worsen over time.

When Sergio was admitted into the Partial Hospital Program, he was living in a foster home. Other than his biological home, this was the longest time he had ever lived in one place—he had been in this home for almost 4 years. Sergio and his other siblings were removed from his biological mother and father when he was approximately 4 years old.

Initially, his removal and subsequent severance from his parents were due to severe neglect and physical abuse. However, once placed in the foster care system, it was obvious that Sergio had experienced significant sexual abuse as well. Sergio was placed with his younger sister in the same home. His foster mother reported that from the first day that they were placed with her, Sergio and his sister continually were engaged in some type of sexualized interactions.

Sergio and his sister's sexual behaviors ranged from exposing themselves to one another, kissing, touching one another's genitals, and humping while dressed. On a couple of occasions, Sergio actually attempted to penetrate his sister while both were fully undressed.

Although the sexual acting out was of the utmost concern, Sergio also exhibited many other problematic behaviors at the time of his placement in the Partial Hospital Program. He had been expelled from his special education classroom on several different occasions for defying staff, physically fighting with other children, assaulting a teacher, cussing and swearing, exposing himself to the class, and on one occasion, urinating in the middle of the classroom.

Later in Sergio's treatment, he was able to disclose some of his memories regarding the abuse he had endured. Sergio reported that his biological father used to beat the children and Sergio with a thorny stick, boards, switches, and his fists. He would berate the children and their mother verbally. Sergio also reported that frequently the family had nothing to eat while his father would go off drinking with friends.

In addition to the abuse mentioned above, Sergio shared some of the sexual abuse he and his siblings were subjected to. He said that his father not only would violate the children by forcing himself on them but also would force the children to have sexual interactions with one another and with their mother.

It was obvious that Sergio was going to need long-term treatment, and even so his prognosis was extremely guarded. He had been a very difficult child in terms of allowing himself to develop any kind of "working" relationship. Frequently, he would lash out physically at the staff when he was beginning to let down his defenses. As with many severely abused children, this was his defense and coping mechanism.

The following session was taken from an individual therapy session approximately 1 year into Sergio's treatment. He had been complaining of frequent nightmares and a great deal of fear when trying to go to sleep. Sergio was asked if he would be willing to draw some pictures that might assist him with sleeping better. He agreed to participate.

Example of Activity #50

At the beginning of the session, Sergio reported his most recent nightmare and discussed how he did not like to go to sleep. This was causing a great deal of stress for Sergio, because he was getting into trouble on a nightly basis with his foster mother, and he was attempting to go into his sister's room in the middle of the night.

Therapist I think we should try something that might help with your nightmares. I want you to think of your most favorite cartoon character.

Sergio What do you mean, like Scooby Doo or the Ninja Turtles?

T That is exactly right. What cartoon character do you think would be able to help you when you had a problem?

S The Ninja Turtles.

T Do you have a favorite turtle?

S Yep, Michelangelo.

T Okay. What we are going to do today is take your dream that you had last night, draw a picture of it, and have Michelangelo help change it.

S Like he's going to be part of my dream?

T Not for real, but in your cartoon he will be a part of your dream. I'm going to split the paper into different squares and then you can draw a cartoon strip of your dream.

S Okay, I can do that.

T In the first box you'll want to start off with your dream.

S (After drawing the picture) This is my dad. He came into my room and started stabbing me with a knife.

T Was this all of your dream, or do you remember more?

S He was saying, "You should never yell at me!"

T Why don't you draw that picture in the next square. What happened next?

S I don't know. . . . That's all I can remember. I think that's when I woke up.

T Okay, well how do you think Michelangelo can help you in your dream?

S He could come into the room and tell my dad, "You should not hurt nobody. These are nice kids. You should never hurt kids anymore."

T That's great. Can you draw that picture in the next square? (Serigo drew the picture.) What do you think would happen next?

S My dad would stab me with the knife.

T Then what would happen?

S   Michelangelo would call for help.

T   What part of that do you want to draw into your cartoon? (Sergio started drawing.)

S   There, this is Michelangelo calling for help. He is saying, "This is Michelangelo. Sergio's dad just hurt him with a knife. Please hurry."

T   So Michelangelo couldn't stop your dad, but he would get help for you afterward, huh? Then what would happen?

S   The ambulance would come. I'm going to draw that.

T   Okay, would anyone say anything?

S   Yeah, Michelangelo would say, "You are not going to die. Your dad will never come out of prison. And you are going to get a new mom and dad that will take care of you."

T   Then what would happen?

S   I would be all better and Michelangelo would come see me in the hospital. I would say, "Thanks for saving me . . ." and he would say, "You are welcome. I'll make sure you don't get hurt again, because you are a great kid!"

Clinical Impressions: This appears to have been a powerful activity for Sergio. He was open and able to process his difficult feelings. The aspect of having a cartoon helper (see Illustration 7.4) to assist him allowed him to create a scenario in which he was able to save himself from his father. The cartoon depicts just how helpless this child felt. The father continued to dominate and stab him, even with a superhero. The damage from his severe history of abuse is so pervasive that this child demonstrates little coping ability. His sense of self seems extremely damaged.

This child continues to live in a psychologically dangerous situation. He fears his father getting out of prison and hurting him. This may never be resolved unless he is able to allow himself to be attached to a new family. However, his deep-seated anger at his father must be resolved first. Otherwise, any new male figure may be projected as his biological father, and Sergio could reject him. He is also a target for continued abuse.

Sergio does wish to have a new family and does want to be seen as a "great" kid. Lots of work must be completed before this will be able to occur.

Illustration 7.4.

This activity does seem to be a good medium for Sergio to use while working through his trauma resolution work. It also may be a useful technique to use his identified cartoon helper, Michelangelo, in other real-life situations. Examples of this might be getting a figurine to keep by his bed at night or a small picture of Michelangelo to keep in his pocket as a reminder that he has a "helper" for difficult day-to-day situations.

❏ **Activity #51: Special Helper to the Rescue!**

Objective: To explore a variety of ways the special helper can assist in problem solving.

This activity is designed to continue the problem-solving process, allowing the child to explore a variety of ways the special helper can assist in solving problems associated with the "monster" identified in Activity #49.

This activity also is intended to allow the child to practice a technique that can be used at home. Therefore, the child's caretakers should be invited to participate in this activity so that they can be more involved in their child's treatment.

Ages: This activity is designed for children ages 6 to 12.

Materials Needed: Activity sheet; pencils, crayons, colored pencils, and/or markers; and additional white paper should be available if needed.

Instructions: Instruct the child to draw about or list three ways that his or her special helper can help with problems. It is important that although the child is drawing the pictures, you need to process how the child sees the "helper" helping him or her with problems. This will help define how the child views the problem-solving process. In the course of your discussion with the child, if the child gives all the power to the helper, you will need to redirect or reframe the process so that the child includes himself or herself, providing a sense of empowerment.

Processing: After the child has completed this activity, it is important to discuss it with him or her by asking, "Tell me about your pictures/list." "How does it feel to have a helper? Why?" "How does it feel to be able to solve problems? Why?"

❑ **Activity #52: Memory Box**

Objective: To make a box for things that are reminders of difficult memories.

This activity is designed to provide a special place to put things that remind the child of difficult memories. This may include pictures of the child's dreams or monsters. For many children, this is a fun activity that encourages creativity and empowerment. They are in charge of designing something that will allow them to feel that the memories are "contained." Some children also will want to make locks to ensure that the boxes are safeguarded.

This may be a difficult time in the healing process, because children often regress when they confront painful memories. They may even feel out of control. Having a special place to contain these painful memories can be beneficial to the child's healing process because it provides a safe structure in which the child can focus his or her thoughts and feelings. This may allow these children to feel more in control.

Ages: Children ages 6 to 12 should have no problems with this activity. The sophistication of the final product created by the child will depend on his or her developmental age.

Materials Needed: Crayons, colored pencils, and/or markers; boxes; glue; and other arts and crafts supplies that encourage creativity.

Instructions: Instruct the child to think about how he or she would like to decorate a box to be used to keep memories safe. Then give the child various sizes of boxes to choose from and ask him or her to choose the kind of box that is needed for those memories.

Once the child has chosen the box, instruct and encourage him or her to decorate it using the supplies provided. As stated above, the actual decorating of the box can be a fun experience. Children usually love to be creative. Therefore, the actual regressive behavior may not manifest itself during this particular activity. However, the box still represents these memories and may elicit some uncomfortable feelings.

Processing: After the child has completed the box, it is important to process the activity by asking, "Tell me about your box." "How did you feel while you were decorating your box?"

❑ Activity #53: Important Memories

Objective: To process various important memories that create certain feelings.

This activity is designed to assist the child in exploring various important memories in his or her life. It is also intended to allow the child to practice expressing his or her memories, linking up thoughts and feelings with particular memories.

The child will be asked to explore his or her first memory as well as the happiest, saddest, and scariest memories. Because exploring can be an extremely difficult task, the child first is asked to start with the less threatening memories, such as the first and happiest memories. The child is then asked to get in touch with more difficult, sad, and frightening memories.

As previously stated in Activity #52, the child may begin showing signs of regression, both behaviorally and emotionally, as he or she begins to get in touch with and link feelings with memories. It will be important for you, as the therapist, to be acutely aware of such signs of regression so that you are able to provide the necessary therapeutic support for the child.

Ages: This activity is designed for children ages 6 to 12.

Materials Needed: Activity sheets and pencils, crayons, colored pencils, and/or markers.

Instructions: Instruct the child to draw pictures of his or her various memories listed on each page. As the child creates a picture, a discussion of the various feelings and aspects associated with the memories should be explored. The child should be encouraged to put the completed pictures in the "memory box" they made in the previous activity.

Note: The older child most likely will have skills to get deeper into this activity, but the younger child will benefit from the experience of exploring various memories through pictures. No matter what age the child is, the child will need to have an understanding of the feelings associated with various life experiences in order to complete this activity successfully.

Processing: After the child has completed each picture, it is important to discuss the feelings associated with that particular memory. We have found it helpful to ask, "Tell me about your picture(s)." "What was your first memory all about? How did you feel about this memory?" "What were your happiest, saddest, and scariest memories all about?" "How did you feel as you drew these memories?" "Which picture was the most comfortable to draw and the most uncomfortable to draw? Why?"

❑ **Activity #54: Things for My Memory Box**

Objective: To collect various items for the memory box.

This activity is designed to give the child the opportunity to continue working through various significant memories in a nonthreatening and fun way. Although the previous activities were more structured and focused on drawing, this activity encourages the child to explore and express important memories, using the child's unique and individual representations for past experiences.

Whereas one child may cut out a picture of a sad, lonely child to represent a memory of a past experience, another child may choose to place a bottle filled with water representing tears in the memory box.

As the child's therapist, you need to be aware that this activity may elicit regression, which may call for more intensive therapeutic intervention. Although it may be difficult for you, as the therapist, to observe the child regressing, this can be a pivotal point in the child's recovery.

As pointed out in the introduction to this chapter, you may find it necessary to consult with a colleague to work through your own countertransference issues if this becomes problematic for you. You also may want to consult with a colleague just to share the intensity of the experience and to bounce ideas off someone who is more objective.

It is important not to allow the intensity of the child's experiences to override the ultimate goal of therapy, which is to work through the memories. Sometimes you may need to provide additional support and take more time to process the intense memories and feelings associated with abusive experiences. It is not recommended that the child's feelings be repressed and nullified at this point in the therapeutic process.

Ages: This activity is designed for children ages 6 to 12.

Materials Needed: Scissors, magazines, pictures, and various other items the child may associate with memories.

Instructions: Instruct the child to look through the various magazines and so forth and start thinking of what is associated with various memories. Then instruct the child to cut out the pictures and pick other items to place in the memory box. As the child is going through the items, have the child discuss how different objects elicit feelings and memories.

This activity may take more than one session. Therefore, you may tell the child to look for various objects to include in the memory box in between sessions.

Note: The child will need to be able to function at a cognitive level that allows him or her to associate various items with memories.

Processing: After the child has collected the items necessary for the memory box, it is important to discuss all the items collected. We have found it helpful to ask, "Tell me about what you have chosen to put in your memory box. Why did you pick each one?" "How did you feel while going through the magazines, etc.?" "Tell me about your feelings and the memories that go with each object you chose."

PHASE III

Repairing the Sense of Self

8

Letting Go of Guilt and Shame

Developmentally, young children are at a stage where they are naturally egocentric, seeing the world from their perspective and assuming others see it the same way. As a result of this unrealistic point of view, they many times mistakenly take on the responsibility for others' actions, even those that have been abusive. When the perpetrator(s) shifts the blame to the child, the child experiences intense feelings of guilt for the abuse (Briere, 1992; Everstine & Everstine, 1989).

There are many other reasons why children blame themselves. They may have been told it was their fault, or their religious beliefs inadvertently may support the idea that sexual experiences outside of wedlock are a "sin"; therefore, these children see themselves participating in a "sinful" act.

If the abuse occurred with a member of the child's immediate family, the child seems to take on more responsibility for the abuse rather than face the reality that the "caregiver(s)" hurt him or her. The child may fear a breakup of the family system or want to protect one parent from the pain that knowledge of the incest would bring. Therefore, the child may feel added pressure to keep the incest or physical abuse a family secret (Briere, 1992).

In addition, children blame themselves for the abuse because they think they should have done something to stop it. They are not able to understand how powerless they are against adults. Unfortunately, the adults or other family members around them frequently blame the child for the abuse. This only adds to and compounds the self-imposed guilt and shame the child already feels.

Young children have a basic need for nurturing. When this need is not met, children will accept any form of closeness, including sexual touching or even physically harsh treatment. At times, sexual molestation physically feels good to children, which only serves to intensify their confusion. It is easy to see how this leads to more guilt and shame and the resultant self-hatred.

Before children can let go of guilt and shame, they must first recognize it, verbalize it, and defuse the power that lies behind it. Admitting shame is the first step in that direction. Secrecy breeds shame. Therefore, as discussed in previous chapters, it is critical for children to develop a trusting relationship so that they are able to share their secrets. This will enable them to emerge from under the cloak of guilt and shame and begin caring for the "child within the child."

Once children are able to defuse the power behind guilt and shame, the next step is to begin the process of grieving and mourning over their losses. There is a sense that they have lost the essence of childhood. However, due to their lack of life experience, they don't even realize what they have lost. This is a critical time in their process of healing.

The goal of this chapter is to assist the child in letting go of the guilt and shame that are at the core of the damaged self. This is probably the most difficult aspect of the healing process. Before the child can truly emerge as a healthy survivor, he or she must let go of the shame, feel the pain, and grieve over the losses. Completing this process allows the disintegrated sense of self to integrate and take shape.

The activities in this chapter will assist the child in addressing the core issues that have created a damaged sense of self. The abused child typically feels responsible for the abuse and harbors enormous feelings of guilt and shame. This can be a trying period in the therapeutic process because the child typically is so entrenched and invested in his or her unhealthy sense of responsibility for the abuse. The psychological position of the child may appear intractable. You may feel like you are on an emotional roller coaster as the child goes through a "push-pull" in letting go of guilt and shame feelings.

As provided in previous chapters, this chapter also contains a few case studies to assist you in further understanding of how some of these activities have been used in actual therapy situations. We have provided a brief case history, an example of dialogue between the therapist and child during the activity, and clinical impressions of the child's work.

You may want to give the child the "Message to the Kids" section for this chapter, which is found in the Activity Book. This will give a brief description of the goals of this chapter. The child can put it in his or her folder or notebook along with other "Messages" and activities already completed.

❑ Activity #55: Jay's Story

Objective: To begin working on feelings associated with abuse, such as guilt and shame.

This activity is designed to introduce the child to the concept of self-blame so commonly felt by abused children. As previously stated, stories are a less threatening medium and can facilitate discussions of difficult feelings. Abused children often feel responsible for their abuse and may harbor enormous feelings of guilt and shame. This story will help the child to identify with another child who feels very similar to how he or she may feel as well as introduce the concept of sharing a secret.

This story may stir up a variety of emotions, central to which is shame. It is very important for children to realize that they can process the feelings of guilt and shame so that the healing process can proceed. This is a difficult process because children really hold onto the belief that they are responsible for the abusive experiences. Unfortunately, this concept is reinforced too often by those who continue to doubt child sexual abuse.

Ages: This activity is appropriate for children ages 6 to 12, provided you read the story to children with reading difficulties.

Materials Needed: Activity sheet and pencils, crayons, colored pencils, and/or markers.

Instructions: Instruct the child to read or listen to Jay's story. After reading the story, instruct the child to complete the questions related to the story. Process the questions with the child.

Note: For children with reading difficulties, the story and questions will need to be read and the child can dictate the answers to you.

Processing: After the child has finished the story, it is important to follow up with a discussion of this story. We have found it helpful to ask, "What do you think about the story?" "How did Jay feel in the story? Why?" "Do you think it was Jay's fault? Why or why not?" "Have you ever felt like Jay? When? Why?"

❏ **Activity #56: My Story**

Objective: To write about the abusive experiences and compile it into a book.

This activity is designed to encourage the child to confront the people who have hurt him or her by drawing pictures of those responsible for the hurt and then either writing or dictating the story about what happened. This is then organized into the child's own storybook.

Because the child already has been talking about secrets and memories, this is the next logical step in putting it all together in a book format. By calling this the child's story, it gives the child an opportunity to express his or her own story from the child's perspective, thus giving the child back some of the power lost when he or she was placed in a victim role.

Ages: This activity is appropriate for children ages 6 to 12.

Materials Needed: Drawing/construction paper; pencils, crayons, markers, and/or colored pencils; extra paper; and paper fasteners, string, or cord.

Instructions: Instruct the child to think about his or her abuse history and label the people responsible for the hurt. Then tell the child to begin either drawing pictures or writing and/or dictating his or her story.

Once the child has completed the story to his or her satisfaction, you may want to reread it together and then encourage the child to design a cover for the book. The final step is to put all of the pages together, including the front and back covers. You can use paper fasteners, string, or cord to complete the book.

Note: The younger child will need more assistance from the therapist regarding direction, dictation, and organization of the book. The child who is more developmentally mature will be able to organize, draw, and write his or her own story with little assistance. You may want to read *Please Tell!* (Jessie, 1991), a story written and illustrated by a little girl who was abused, to use as a model prior to engaging in this activity.

Processing: After the child has completed the book, it is important to go through the entire book and process it by asking, "Tell me about your book. Do you want to read it?" "What did it feel like telling your story?" "How do you feel putting your story in a book or on paper? Why?"

Case Example: *Donna*

Brief Case History: This case was discussed in Chapter 2 (Activity #2). Briefly, Donna was a 7-year-old with a history of severe sexual abuse by multiple perpetrators while living with her mother and her mother's boyfriend. She appeared to have been exposed to satanic, ritualistic abuse. Donna also had begun perpetrating on other children.

Donna was attractive, precocious, and acted "parentified" and pseudomature as she described her abuse history and her own sexual acting-out behavior.

After being at the hospital several months, it was decided to have Donna make an "Abuse Book." She found this activity very helpful because she processed a myriad of feelings while completing this project. It was a good way to help her put together all the information she had been sharing in her therapy. After completing this book, she continually referred to it in later sessions.

Example of Activity #56

The following is a dialogue that went on while she was going through her completed book. Only the first session will be discussed, because it took many sessions to complete this activity.

Therapist   Donna, how about making a book about all the different people who hurt you and how you felt about it? We could include some of the pictures you already did.

Donna   I like that idea. We could use the one I did of all the people who touched me for the first page.

T   That's a good idea. I know you have already drawn a picture of all the different people who have hurt you. Is that where you want to start?

D   No, I want to start by drawing a picture for the cover of my book and put the title on it.

T   Okay. What do you want to call your book?

D   I want to write, "Abuse, by Donna." How do you spell abuse?

T   A-b-u-s-e.

D   Okay. Now I want to color it.

After the book cover was completed, Donna wanted to include the picture she already drew of her various perpetrators. At this point, Donna proceeded to draw pictures of her mother's boyfriend and her aunt with little difficulty. Then she dictated something about each of these people. Donna refused to work anymore on her book that day and began exhibiting difficulty on the unit (in the hospital). The following is from the second session on her book.

T   Last time we met, you wanted to stop after drawing a picture of your aunt. What do you want to do now?

D   I want to draw a picture of my mom, but this is hard.

T   I'm sure it is . . .

D   But I can do it. (Donna proceeds to draw a picture of her mother.)

T   Okay, what do you want me to write under her picture?

D   Write down, "I don't like her. She is not a good mom or she wouldn't have sexually abused me. She abused every single one of my cousins. I saw what she did to them. She hurt Curtis, Paul, Chuck, Rose, Holly, Carol, and a girl with brown hair and brown eyes who is tiny. She threatened to kill me if I told."

T   Anything else?

D   Yes. Write that "my mom broke my heart once because she gave me a puppy once. Then she took the puppy back and gave it to someone else. It broke my heart because I fell in love with that puppy right away. It made me mad that she took it away from me."

T   I bet it did.

D   I really don't want to do anymore today.

Donna proceeded to start singing spontaneously, as she often did in her individual therapy sessions with her primary therapist.

Clinical Impressions: This activity took place after a few months in a subacute inpatient hospital program. She had almost daily individual therapy sessions and daily group sessions. Donna had progressed fairly well in therapy. She was an engaging, bright, young girl.

This activity was spread over several sessions. She ended up with a 10-page book (see Illustrations 8.1, 8.2, and 8.3) of the people who had abused her and her feelings associated with each one. Donna's picture and story about her mother giving her a puppy and then taking it back seem like a good analogy of her own life experiences.

Donna had moved back and forth from mom to dad. She was then sent to the hospital, sent back home briefly, and then rehospitalized when she disclosed that she had sexually molested a little boy (this was later found out to be a fabrication so that she could return to the hospital where she felt safe).

According to Terr (1994), creative children sometimes dissociate as a form of pretending. This may take the form of dancing and singing. This was apparent in Donna's case. She often would break out in song, as if she were starring in a Broadway musical, as she did at the end of the second session mentioned above. At times, it was eerie when she did this in the middle of a therapy session. It occurred only in individual sessions when she appeared to be overwhelmed by her traumatic memories and feelings associated with these memories.

Donna exhibited both Type I and Type II symptoms of trauma, according to Terr's (1994, p. 11) description. When her puppy was taken away, she exhibited tremendous detail of the event (Type I trauma). However, when describing her various sexual molests, she would often confuse what happened on which occasion but was very clear on the identity of the person (Type II trauma).

Although this activity was difficult for her and at times did escalate her behavior problems on the unit and at school, Donna did benefit from completing this task. She seemed pleased with herself and proud of the completed book. Her behavior problems did subside and she was able to gain more control over her impulsive, sexualized behavior.

Donna's trauma history was so extensive that her stay in the subacute program was only the beginning of a long-term process toward recovery. Although her prognosis is guarded without exten-

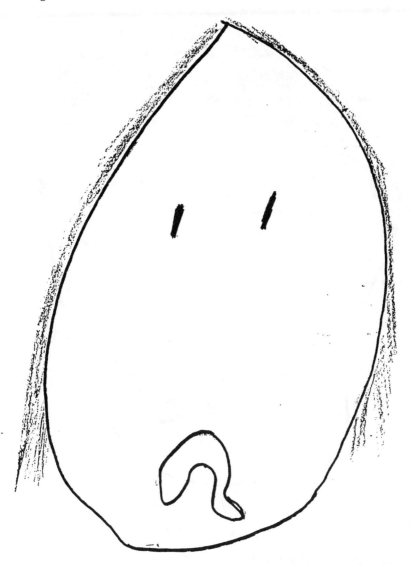

Illustration 8.1.

sive therapy, the early intervention will give her a better chance of
a positive resolution to her trauma.

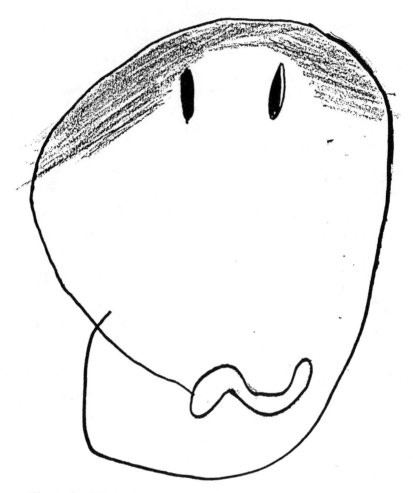

Illustration 8.2.

❏ **Activity #57: I Would Say . . .**

Objective: To confront the abuser(s) by means of drawing a picture and writing about being hurt.

This activity is designed to begin the process of addressing the child's response to his or her abuse. It is important for the child to confront the abuser(s), express his or her feelings about the abuse,

Illustration 8.3.

and make statements directed toward the person(s) who hurt the child. However, it is not necessary for the child to "personally" or "physically" confront the abuser(s).

This activity begins the process of confronting the abuser(s), not just the abuse. It allows the child to do so in a nonthreatening way by using a medium—storytelling—that is typically fun.

This may be difficult for some children to do, but other children will use this as a forum to gain "power" by exaggerating and inflating their responses. For example, some children may state, "I'll kill you if you ever hurt me again." Some children may get very detailed on how they would accomplish this.

It is important for you, as the child's therapist, to understand that this is just the child's way of attempting to gain "power" that was taken from him or her by the abuser. The child is attempting to move from a sense of powerlessness to a position of having some control. You will need to process the reality of the child's statements, assisting him or her to separate wishes and desires from what is real.

Ages: This activity is appropriate for children who are at a stage, developmentally, in which they have enough ego strength to confront the abuser(s) with their feelings. Some children as young as 6 are able to complete this activity relatively easily.

Materials Needed: Activity sheet and pencils, crayons, markers, and/or colored pencils.

Instructions: Instruct the child to reread his or her story; some children may either choose or need you to read it to them. Then tell the child to draw a picture of the person(s) who hurt them. Once the child has completed the picture(s), encourage the child to think about and state what he or she would like to say to the person(s) about being hurt.

It is important for the child to put his or her words in writing. Writing the words moves the feelings from being intangible to being more concrete because the child is taking the thoughts and feelings from within and putting them on paper. It is another step toward empowerment.

Note: Be aware that even children with stable enough ego strength may show signs of regression because this activity taps into their guilt and shame.

Processing: After the child has completed the picture and statement about the abuse, it is important to discuss the picture and feelings by asking, "Tell me about your picture." "What did you tell the person(s) in your picture(s)? Is there anything else you want to say to the person(s)? What?" "How does it feel to express your feelings to the person(s) who hurt you? Why?"

❑ Activity #58: Thinking It Was My Fault

Objective: To begin addressing guilt and shame associated with abuse by looking at self-blame.

Although the child has been introduced to the concept that abuse is not the child's fault, this is a difficult concept to get across. Therefore, you, as the child's therapist, will need to address this over and over again.

When children think abuse is their fault, they incorporate guilt and shame feelings around the abuse. They begin to feel intense shame that is difficult to let go. One place to start is to have the child begin to address how he or she has come to think it was his or her fault. This allows the child to confront "faulty" thinking. This activity begins the *cognitive restructuring* process of the child's faulty or mistaken belief system.

Ages: This activity is designed for children ages 6 to 12 as long as they are developmentally able to read the sentences and finish them.

Instructions: Instruct the child to read the sentences and complete them, stating why it feels like the abuse was his or her fault. If the child has problems reading or understanding the words, read and discuss the sentences. Examples may be used about how the child has felt something was his or her fault in the past (i.e., breaking someone's toy by accident). It also may be necessary to have the child dictate the response to you.

Note: For younger children, it may be necessary to read the sentences to them and have them dictate how they would finish the sentences.

Materials Needed: Activity sheet and pencils.

Processing: After the child has completed the sentences, it is important to go over each one and discuss the responses. With a very
verbal child, this may be enough. For some children, we have found
it helpful to ask, "How do you feel about your sentences? Why?"
"What does *fault* mean to you?" "Was this activity hard or easy for
you? Why?"

The following case example will illustrate how one abused child
processed this activity.

Case Example: *Amy*

Brief Case History: Amy's case was discussed in Chapter 3 (Activity
#12). Briefly, Amy had a history of physical, emotional, and sexual
abuse by her mother and her numerous boyfriends. During one visit
to her mother (while in foster care), Amy was kidnapped by her
mother, who took Amy to a different state, changed her name, and
dyed her hair.

This girl has suffered severe trauma due to the abuse and kidnapping. She also had a disrupted adoption attempt.

This activity was completed after Amy had been in the Child
Residential Program for several months. She had been struggling
with feelings of guilt, and it was decided to use cognitive restructuring in an attempt to help her sort out her feelings. Therefore,
Activities #58 and #59 were done in one session. The following
dialogue was during the discussion of Activity #58.

Example of Activity #58

Therapist Amy, we've talked about how you are always blaming
yourself for the times you were hurt.
Amy Yeah.
T I want you to finish these sentences so we can see why you
sometimes believe it was your fault. Then we'll talk about them.
Okay?

After Amy completed her sentences, she wanted to read them to
the therapist.

A   Okay. Well, first of all I thought it was my fault because I thought I should have been able to get away from it.

T   Okay.

A   Number 2, sometimes I believe it was my fault because I thought I deserved it when my dad slammed me on the chair.

T   I think we'll need to talk about these. . . . Go ahead.

A   Number 3, sometimes I believe it was my fault because my sister did not believe me when I told her that I was molested by Mom's boyfriend.

T   So you blamed yourself for that?

A   Yes. Number 4, sometimes I believe it was my fault because when I got taken away from my mom I thought it was my fault—I wasn't good enough.

As soon as Amy finished this paper, the next paper, with Activity #59, was given to her, and an explanation of changing her last statements to more positive statements was discussed. Clinical impressions will be given at the end of Activity #59.

❑ Activity #59: It Really Wasn't My Fault

Objective: To learn a cognitive restructuring technique to counter negative self-statements.

This activity is designed to piggyback on the last activity so that the child can follow up with a more reality-based response to why abuse is not really the child's fault. This process also is referred to as cognitive restructuring. It is very difficult for children to truly believe that it was not their fault, just as they often believe that their parents' divorce was their fault.

This activity will take lots of discussion before the child will be able to complete the sentences. The child needs to process why abuse is not a child's fault, in general. Then, maybe the child will be able to move more specifically to his or her own issues.

Ages: Children who are developmentally able to discuss the concept of fault should be able to complete this activity.

Materials Needed: Activity sheet and pencils.

Instructions: Instruct the child to complete the sentences after the discussion regarding fault. It may be necessary to read the sentences and let the child dictate the responses.

Note: Some children may need assistance by reading the sentences to them and having them dictate their responses. It is also important to note that usually Activities #58 and #59 are completed together so the child can see how his or her negative, faulty thinking can be changed.

Processing: After the child completes this activity (and the one prior), they should be processed together. We have found it helpful to ask, "How do you feel about your sentences? Why?" "Why isn't it children's fault when they are abused? Why?" "Was this activity easy or difficult to complete? Why?"

Example of Activity #59

The following example of Activity #59 is a continuation from Activity #58 (see case example from the previous activity). When Amy finished Activity #58, she was given Activity #59 to complete after a discussion of thinking errors.

Therapist Amy, now I want you to go back and look at your sentences about how you sometimes think it was your fault. Let's take a good look at each one.

Amy Okay.

T Look at #1—do you really think you should have gotten away? Think of how young you were and how big Mom's boyfriends were.

A I see what you mean. I can change the sentence to how it wasn't my fault.

T Right! How would you change that?

A   Well, I was not big. My mom's boyfriends were way too big and too strong for me to get away from them.

T   I agree with you. Now that's more like it. I want you to finish the rest of these sentences.

After Amy finished the sentences, she wanted to read them to the therapist.

A   Number 2, it was not my fault because my dad should have had his control before hurting me like that. I never deserve being hurt in any way.

T   I agree! That's a great way to change your other sentence. Why did you think you deserved it at the time?

A   Well, I wasn't listening to him, but I have been learning how to keep my control and he was an adult. He should know about that.

T   Just because you weren't listening to him isn't a reason to hurt you. I'm glad you can see that now.

A   Number 3, it was not my fault because my sister did not believe me when I told her about the molest. I know that it had happened to me. I shouldn't have worried that she didn't believe me. I guess I started wondering if it ever happened, but I know it did.

T   I'm glad you're beginning to trust yourself.

A   Number 4, it was not my fault because she had lots of chances and blew them to have me in the house with her. I know that I am good. I still miss her, though.

T   Of course you do. It's not easy to be taken away from your mother. That's going to be a hard one for you to completely deal with. You talk a lot about wanting to see your mother again.

A   Yeah, but then I get really angry and say I don't ever want to see her again. I get so frustrated.

T   I can imagine. How did you feel while you did this activity?

A   I felt good about changing my other sentences. I don't really want to blame myself, but sometimes I do.

T   Amy, should children be blamed for their abuse?

A   No. They're only little. Parents are supposed to take care of their children and protect them. My mom didn't protect me from her boyfriends. That's why she lost me.

Soon after that, the session ended. Amy seemed very proud of herself for how she was able to change her negative, self-blaming sentences into acknowledging how it was *not* her fault.

Clinical Impressions: The sentences pretty much reflect how Amy felt about herself at the time she was being abused. Both activities reflect the "push-pull" she goes through continually. She defends her mother and then rejects her. She blames herself for the abuse by her father and then seems to "intellectually" see that it is not her fault.

Amy is a typical example of a child who has been severely scarred by her traumatic history. She was subjected to a mother who exposed her to her many boyfriends (who molested her) as well as her mom's life as a prostitute. Then her mother kidnapped her and changed her name. Following that, she was molested while in foster care. This child does not know who to trust, for good reason.

The two activities were completed during one session so that Amy would not be left with her "faulty" thinking. It was decided that it would be better for her to challenge these thinking errors and restructure them into more reality-based cognitions.

Amy responded very well to this approach. She seemed to enjoy the challenge to her "thinking errors" and the confirmation that she was not at fault. In fact, a copy was given to her so that whenever she made these statements to herself she could look back and see how to challenge this way of thinking.

This approach of cognitive restructuring will need to be done many times with Amy. This will help her integrate a new belief system into her repertoire so that she will continue to build a stronger and more positive sense of self.

❏ Activity #60: Me—Before and After

Objective: To evaluate the damage done to the self by drawing the self before the hurt and after being hurt.

This activity is designed to assist children in seeing how they perceived themselves before and during the abusive period in their life. This may be a concrete activity for some children, meaning they may draw a picture of themselves as a baby and then a bit older. However, for other children, this can be a deeper, more revealing activity. They may draw a young child looking happy and content and then draw a "damaged" child who is quite sad, hurt, or angry. Parts of their body may even look "damaged."

Ages: Children of all ages should be able to complete this activity.

Materials Needed: Activity sheet and pencils, crayons, colored pencils, and/or markers.

Instructions: Instruct the child to first draw a picture of himself or herself before the hurt happened. Then have the child draw a picture of the "hurt self." Make sure the child labels which picture is the "hurt self."

Note: As mentioned above, the younger, less mature child may approach this activity very concretely and just draw different stages of development (big and small). Older or more mature children will tend to get more involved in this activity and put feelings, captions, and so on into their drawings.

Processing: After the child has drawn the before and after pictures, it is important to discuss the drawings. We have found it helpful to ask, "Tell me about the picture of yourself before you were hurt." "How do you feel in this picture? Why?" "Tell me about the picture of your hurt self." "How do you feel in this picture? Why?" "How did you feel while drawing each of your pictures? Why?"

❏ **Activity #61: "Lost" Things**

Objective: To discuss the many "losses" from abuse.

   This activity is designed to allow the child to explore the sense of loss that often occurs when a child has been abused. Children who have been abused often grow up before their time. They may forget how to play or they may never have had the opportunity to learn how to play and be a kid.

The loss for some abused children may be very evident, such as being placed in foster homes and/or being put up for adoption. To these children, the concept of loss is fairly easy to understand because it is so concrete and real.

Ages: This activity is most appropriate for the older child who has a better understanding of the concept of loss, possibly age 11 or 12.

Materials Needed: Activity sheet and pencils.

Instructions: Prior to starting this activity, it might be a good idea to have a discussion with the child about the concept of "loss" as it relates to being damaged. It will be important to review things such as feeling "too grown-up" when they were supposed to enjoy being a "kid," the loss of a family if the family has been separated due to the abuse allegations, and the sadness and guilt that some children feel resulting from the abuse.

Instruct the child to think about the things he or she has lost or that are gone because of the abuse. Then have the child either write or dictate these losses. While the child is working on this activity, you may need to ask, "Are there any other things you can think of?" because the child may be somewhat resistant to think about his or her losses.

This sense of loss can become quite overwhelming for the child; therefore it will be important for you, as the therapist, to frequently "check in" and process with the child throughout this activity.

Note: If the loss is profound, as stated above, the younger child may be able to successfully complete this activity. We have found that children as young as 7 or 8, who have been permanently removed from their home, easily identify the feeling of loss in regard to "losing their family."

Processing: After the child has completed the list, it is important to discuss the list by asking, "Tell me about your list of lost things."

"Which thing on your list is the hardest for you? Why?" "How did you feel writing your list? Why?"

❏ Activity #62: My Letter

Objective: To learn how to comfort the hurt child within by writing a letter to the hurt child.

This activity is designed to allow the child to address the hurt feelings resulting from the abusive experience(s). It is important for children to recognize the hurt child within the child and validate their feelings. Therefore, one very effective way to address this is to write a therapeutic letter to the hurt child within.

Writing therapeutic letters has been found to be an excellent way to confront difficult feelings (Bass & Davis, 1988). It allows the child abuse survivor to be more direct in confronting these feelings rather than just talking about these feelings.

Ages: Most children can relate to being hurt. Therefore, this activity is appropriate for children ages 6 to 12. The only criterion is that the child is able to identify feelings.

Materials Needed: Activity sheet and pencils.

Instructions: Instruct the child to either write or dictate a letter to his or her hurt child.

Note: The younger or delayed child may need to dictate his or her letter to you.

Processing: After the child has written the letter to the hurt child, it is important to process the letter by asking, "How did it feel to write your letter? Why?" "Tell me about your hurt child." "Is there anything else you would like to add?"

The following case example will illustrate how one young trauma victim processed this activity.

Case Example: *Armando*

Brief Case History: Armando was a 9-year-old who lived with his mother, father, and 3-year-old sister. Armando was placed in the Partial Hospital Program by his school district after several episodes of violent outbursts in his self-contained classroom setting.

Armando was described as always being impulsive, angry, and very aggressive toward others. His violent outbursts were directed not only toward people but also toward the family dog and inanimate objects both at home and in his school. Armando had been physically abused on one occasion when his father threw him against the wall. This occurred when Armando attempted to stop his father from beating his mother.

The majority of Armando's traumatic experiences came from observing the violent domestic fights between his mother and father. It seemed this had been occurring for the majority of his life. Armando's mother had gone to the hospital for medical attention after several of the altercations.

The following example was from a session with Armando in which he wrote a letter to his parents regarding their behaviors and his desire for change. This activity allowed Armando to feel more empowered in his own healing process and gave a clear message to his parents. Initially, Armando was reluctant to give the letter directly to his parents because of fear of retaliation from his father; however, at the end of the session, he asked that the letter be brought and read in the next family session. In reading the letter at the family session, Armando's father committed to begin his own treatment to deal with his addiction to alcohol and to engage in therapy for anger management.

Example of Activity #62

Therapist Okay, Armando, we had decided that we would work on that letter to your parents today. Are you ready to get started?

Armando Yeah, but I don't write very good.

T   Well, if you want I can be your secretary. I'll just write down everything you say. When you are finished you can decide if you want to copy it over in your own writing or if you want to put it on the computer.

A   Okay.

T   How do you want to start your letter?

A   What do you mean?

T   Well, who are you writing your letter to?

A   My mom and dad, you know that.

T   How do you want to start your letter. Dear Mom and Dad . . . or just Mom and Dad . . . or would you like to start it some other way?

A   No, I want to start it by saying, "Dear Mom and Dad."

T   Okay. Then, what do you want me to write? Remember, you want to tell them how you are feeling with their fighting.

A   I want you to write, "I have gotten to the point where I can't take your fighting anymore. It makes me angry because I just don't understand why you fight. At school they let me know fighting isn't okay, but when I come home there is lots of fighting. Good willpower can take away the fighting. You can do the best for yourselves because it's the best for me."

T   Armando, you have done a wonderful job of telling your parents how angry their fighting makes you feel and what you would like them to do about it. Is there anything else you would like to say in your letter or other feelings you need to let them know about?

A   I want you to write that "when you guys fight I feel very, very angry because there is not happiness in your fights. I wish for the madness to go away so that you feel so happy that you don't have to fight anymore."

T   Do you want to end your letter, or do you want to add more to it?

A   What do you think? Do you think it's okay the way that it is?

T   I think it's a very good letter. You have told your parents their fighting makes you angry, that you wish it would stop, and that you want people in your home to be happy. Is this all that you want to say to your parents?

A   No. I want to tell them that I feel scared when they fight because I think someone is going to get hurt.

T   So you want me to write, "I feel scared when you fight because I think one of you are going to get hurt."

A   Yep, and I want you to write, "I wish you would do the best for yourselves because it isn't happy for me. Your fighting is ruining your lives and it's ruining my life. I'm trying to tell you how I feel and what your fighting does to my life."

T   Wow, Armando, you have done a great job with your letter. You are very brave to be able to tell your feelings about your parents fighting. How do you want to finish your letter?

A   What do you mean? I've said everything that I want to. My letter is finished.

T   I know and you have done a fantastic job. Sometimes people sign letters and cards by saying: Sincerely, and then your name; or Love, and then your name. You know, something like that. You don't have to. I'm just asking if you want to sign it.

A   Yeah, I want to sign it, "Love, your son."

T   Okay, Armando. You can decide what you want to do with your letter. You can keep it for yourself, or you can give it to your parents. Whatever you want to do is fine. How does it feel to have written a letter to your mom and dad, letting them know how their fighting makes your feel?

A   Well, it kind of makes me feel proud of myself that I am being brave enough to tell them how their fighting makes me feel. But I'm kind of scared, too, because I am not sure how they will feel when they read it. I don't want them to get mad because I've been talking about it.

T   I think you are very brave, Armando, and you are doing a great job of taking care of yourself and your feelings. You don't have to give the letter to your parents if you don't want to. Remember, writing the letter was for you to take care of yourself.

A   I know, but I kind of would like them to read it because I want them to stop. Maybe by seeing how it makes me feel they will stop doing it, and things can be happy at my house.

T   It's up to you, Armando. Whatever you decide to do is fine with me. If you think I can help somehow, just let me know and I will do my best.

A   Do you think you can give this letter to my parents? Maybe they won't get so mad if you give it to them.

T   Sure, I can do that. What if I bring it to my next home visit? I don't think your parents will be that mad, Armando. Your mom and dad have told me a lot of times that they want you to talk about anything that is upsetting to you. Your parents just want you to be happier.

A   Well, I would be happier if they would just quit fighting so much.

T   Maybe you would be able to stop fighting with people easier if there wasn't as much fighting going on at home, huh? You know, just like you would like your parents to stop fighting, everyone else would like you to stop fighting, too. Fighting never makes any one feel happy.

The session ended soon after that.

Clinical Impressions: Although Armando presents as a rather strange child with psychotic features, he seemed to respond to this activity with a clear goal.

Armando was able to state his feelings clearly regarding his parents' behavior. He was able to state his wish for change and appeared to benefit from putting his thoughts into writing (see Illustration 8.4).

For many children, getting thoughts and feelings into a more concrete form is very beneficial. Armando had perseverated about this problem for so long that he seemed relieved to finally put it on paper. There was a definite decrease in his violent behavior in other settings (e.g., the classroom) following this activity.

The dialogue between the therapist and Armando reveals the difficulty he had when it came to his decision to present his letter in a family session. The letter appeared to give him a sense of empowerment and yet seemed to set up a conflict. In his particular family (as in many others), family matters were not discussed outside the family. Breaking the code of family secrecy was risky for the child.

In this case, Armando was the one to decide that he wanted his parents to see his letter. The therapist makes it clear that he does not need to show his parents his letter. In fact, she points out that the letter is for him. His compromise is to have the therapist read the letter in the next family session.

Dear Mom and Dad,

I have gotten to the point where I can't take your fighting anymore.
It makes me angry because I just don't understand why you fight. At
school they let me know fighting isn't okay, but when I come home
there is lots of fighting. Good willpower can take away the fighting.
You can do the best for yourselves because it's the best for me.

When you guys fight I feel very, very angry because there is not
happiness in your fights. I wish for the madness to go away so that
you feel so happy that you don't have to fight anymore.

I feel scared when you fight because I think one of you are going to
get hurt.

I just wish you would do the best for yourselves because it isn't happy
for me. Your fighting is ruining your lives and it's ruining my life. I'm
trying to tell you how I feel and what your fighting does to my life.

Love,

Your son

Illustration 8.4.

Clinically, this case is reflective of how many children growing up
in families where there is domestic violence feel the need to "fix" the
family. This puts the child in a parentified position and can give a
false sense of power.

9

Working Through
the "Stuck" Feelings

Once children have begun to work through the guilt and shame and
have allowed themselves to address the feelings related to their
losses, other repressed feelings may begin to surface. It is important
to work through these "stuck" feelings.

Typically children get "stuck" as they begin to feel anger, hurt,
fear, and pain due to their concrete way of viewing the world as
good or bad. Children tend to view themselves as good or bad
people rather than separating their self-worth from their feelings.

As we stated in Chapter 3, it is healthy and normal to experience
a variety of feelings. However, we suggest they be viewed as comfortable and safe or uncomfortable, unsafe, or difficult feelings
rather than good or bad. The more you can help children accept their
feelings without judgment, the easier it will be for them to recognize
and work through the "stuck" feelings.

In addition, it is important to help children understand that their
experiences and the resultant feelings are separate from their sense
of self-worth. Bad experiences do not make bad children. However,

most children will continue to label their abuser as bad and the experience as bad. Allow the child to do that if it helps him or her get in touch with angry feelings.

Bass and Davis (1988) so aptly refer to anger as "the backbone of healing." Anger serves as an effective motivator to respond and act. Allowing themselves to feel angry counteracts the tendency for children to slip into feelings of hopelessness, despair, and self-blame.

Children will often use anger as a defense mechanism to mask underlying feelings of fear, hurt, and pain. They tend to use anger in diffuse ways because they respond to their world in a reactive, chaotic manner rather than focusing their energy on the underlying, painful feelings that have been created by their abusers. In this respect, children are not so unlike their adult counterparts who have not completely worked through abuse histories, operating from a base of anger.

If anger is to be effective, it must be expressed appropriately and focused at those who have hurt them and have not kept them safe. When anger is turned inward, children become depressed, self-destructive, and filled with self-blame, which becomes self-hate. However, when children outwardly misdirect their anger, they tend to get out of control, and anything in their path, including themselves and others, becomes "fair game."

Confronting the abuse is a necessary aspect of healing. However, confrontation does not necessarily require a direct encounter with the perpetrator(s) or the caregiver(s) who have not kept the child safe. The necessity is to confront the underlying feelings that were created by the abuse. This may lead to direct or indirect confrontations with the individual(s) responsible for the pain and suffering the child has incurred.

The purpose of this chapter is to help the child work through "stuck" feelings. This includes several goals, such as identifying underlying feelings, appropriately expressing these feelings, working through anger, and confronting those responsible for the pain. Successfully completing this phase of the healing process allows children to achieve an integration of their life experiences and feelings of self-worth so they are ready to become "healthy survivors."

The activities in this chapter are designed to assist the child in working through feelings such as anger, hurt, and pain that often surface after the child has worked through the guilt and shame. This can be a very energized time, because children can become more focused and empowered in directing their feelings more appropriately.

As done in previous chapters, this chapter also contains a few case studies to assist you in further understanding of how some of these activities have been used in actual therapy situations. We have given a brief case history, an example of dialogue between the therapist and child during the activity, and clinical impressions of the child's work.

Again, it is recommended to give the child a copy of the "Message to the Kids" for this chapter so the child has a brief explanation of the goals of this chapter.

❑ Activity #63: My Sad Feelings

Objective: To continue processing any additional sad feelings yet unresolved.

This activity is designed to allow children to continue processing any additional sad feelings that they still may be experiencing. After children have worked through various stages of their recovery, they may have additional feelings that are not yet resolved, or new feelings may emerge.

It is important to encourage the child to continue the process of exploring various feelings. This activity and the next two activities are designed for this purpose. It is hoped that with this additional structured practice, the child will incorporate this critical skill into his or her everyday life.

Ages: This activity is designed for children ages 6 to 12. Any child that has the capacity to identify and express his or her feelings will find this activity useful.

Materials Needed: Activity sheet and pencils, crayons, markers, and/or colored pencils.

Instructions: Instruct the child to think about the things that are still making sad feelings. Then have the child draw pictures or list these things. Once the child has identified the specific things creating sad feelings, instruct him or her to complete the "I feel" statements.

Note: The younger child may choose to draw pictures and need assistance in completing the "I feel" statements.

Processing: After the child has completed this activity, it is important to process the statements (or pictures) by asking, "Tell me about the things that are still making sad feelings for you." "What do you want to do with these sad feelings?" "Tell me about your 'I feel' statements."

❏ Activity #64: My Scary Feelings

Objective: To continue processing scary feelings that are as yet unresolved.

This activity is designed to explore scary feelings that are yet unresolved. As in the previous activity, many children need to continue the process of exploring difficult feelings. (See previous activity for more detailed explanation.)

Materials Needed: Activity sheet and pencils, markers, crayons, and/or colored pencils.

Instructions: Instruct the child to think about the things that are still making scary feelings. Then have the child either draw pictures or list the things that still make him or her afraid. Once the child has identified the specific things creating scary feelings, have him or her complete the "I feel" statements.

Processing: After the child is finished with this activity, it is important to process the lists (or pictures) by asking, "Tell me about the things that still make you feel afraid." "What do you want to do with these scary feelings?" "Tell me about your 'I feel' statements."

The following case example will illustrate how one abused girl processed this activity.

Case Example: *Samantha*

Brief Case History: This case was discussed in Chapter 3, Activity #13. Briefly, Samantha was a 7-year-old who was referred for outpatient therapy for problems relating to domestic violence. She was the oldest of two children, having a 4-year-old sister.

At the time of referral, Samantha was experiencing several post-traumatic effects, such as intense fear, agitated behavior, scary dreams, flashbacks, difficulty falling asleep, hypervigilance, and startle response. She was somewhat obsessed with her father's drinking pattern and expressed worried feelings about others' drinking. She felt that drinking alcohol generally led to violence.

Therapy focused on the fears Samantha described and her sense of helplessness. She found it difficult to express angry feelings, most likely due to her father's out-of-control anger. Although fear and scared feelings were not difficult for her to express, she seemed "stuck" in this mode. It was decided that it would be helpful to go back and have her draw a picture of the incident that brought her into therapy.

Example of Activity #64

Samantha was instructed to draw a picture of the incident that scared her before she came into therapy (see Illustration 9.1). We then discussed her drawing. She was asked to use "I feel" statements as she described her feelings. As Samantha stated her "I feel" statements, the therapist wrote them down.

Therapist Samantha, tell me about your drawing.
Samantha Well, this is a picture of my dad pushing my mom into that table.
T Tell me about how each one of you feels. Why don't you start with you—how do you feel, using "I feel" statements.

Dad   Mom   Samantha

Illustration 9.1.

S   Well, I am crying here. I feel frightened.

T   How about your mom and dad?

S   Well, my mom is crying, too. She feels sad. Here is my dad. He feels mad.

T   Look at this little girl (referring to Samantha), how else does she feel?

S   Scared?

T   Is that how you felt?

S   Yeah. I felt so bad because I couldn't do anything to stop him.

T   You felt helpless?

S   Yes. That's just how I felt. I couldn't help my mom or my sister.

T   But you did yell for someone who could help, didn't you?

S   Yes. . . . I called for Fred and Sally, our neighbors, but my dad wouldn't let go of my little sister. My mom tried to take her away so we could go next door. My dad was drunk and he wouldn't let go. This worried me. I didn't know what he would do with her. She's only 4. I kept crying.

T   Are you still worried about that happening again?

S   Sort of. . . . I really don't think my dad will ever do that again, but if he drinks alcohol again, I'm worried he'll get real angry.

T   Then what do you think would happen?

S   I think Mom would take us and leave for a while.

T   Where would you go?

S   Probably to Grandma and Grandpa's house.

T   So you think your mom would be able to leave before a fight happened?

S   Yeah. I think she would leave instead of yelling at him. That's when he used to get angry. If she started yelling at him for drinking.

T   So now your mother realizes she has no control over your father's drinking, and so she wouldn't yell. She would just take you to your grandparents?

S   Yeah. But I hope that never happens.

T   I realize that. It seems that everyone is working so hard on making things better now. Maybe that won't happen.

S   I hope not.

The session ended soon after that. The mother verified that they were still in marital therapy and doing well.

Clinical Impressions: It appears that Samantha is still stuck in her fears related to the domestic violence incident. However, she has progressed in her ability to verbalize her fears in more detail. She also seems to feel that things may work out, but if things start to become a problem, she feels Mom would remove them from the situation. This is a much healthier situation.

It is important to note that the mom and dad are progressing very well in marital therapy with a colleague. We have received permission to confer on this case. Therefore, she is able to help the parents work on issues that pertain to Samantha's fears. This can also pave the way for goals in family therapy.

Samantha is doing well in her ability to process her feelings of helplessness, and now sees her mother as the one to take care of her and her sister. In the past, she seemed to feel responsible for "fixing" things. This is definitely an improvement.

❏ **Activity #65: My Angry Feelings**

Objective: To continue processing angry feelings that are unresolved.
    This activity is designed to assist the child in processing unfinished angry feelings. (See Activity #63 for further information.)

Materials Needed: Activity sheet and pencils, markers, crayons, and/or colored pencils.

Instructions: Instruct the child to think about the things that still make him or her feel angry. Then have the child either draw pictures or list the things that still make him or her angry. Once the child has completed this step, instruct him or her to complete the "I feel" statements.

Processing: After the child has completed this activity, it is important to discuss the lists (or pictures) by asking, "Tell me about the things that still make you feel angry." "What do you want to do with your angry feelings?" "Tell me about your 'I feel' statements."
    The following case example will illustrate how one abused and neglected child processed this activity.

Case Example: *Danny*

Brief Case History: Danny was an 8-year-old who was living with his biological mother when he was referred to the Partial Hospital Program for intensive treatment for his out-of-control behaviors. Danny's biological father died from a drug overdose shortly after he was born.
    Danny was referred to the Partial Hospital Program after he had made several threats to hurt himself and on one occasion attempted to hang himself with a belt in his home. Initially, it was difficult to ascertain whether Danny's actions were an outcome of suicidal

ideation or whether they resulted from out-of-control attention-seeking behaviors and defiance.

In addition to Danny's threats of self-harm, he exhibited a great deal of out-of-control and assaultive behaviors in all of his settings. In his public school setting, he had been assaultive to his peers and made several threats to his teachers. He had been expelled from school on several occasions because he would purposely trip, kick, hit, and push other children. He also would use bad language, swear, throw things, refuse to follow directions, and was basically defiant with any authority figure.

In his home, Danny was also out of control. He frequently would throw temper tantrums that included yelling, kicking, swearing, hitting, throwing things, breaking things, and refusing to do anything his mother asked of him. Danny's mother had all but given up on him and was at the point where she did not even like to be around him.

Initially, Danny's history of abuse was somewhat vague. Although his mother did admit to hitting him with a belt and other objects when he was younger, she said she had not done this for years. She did continue to "threaten" Danny with such actions if he did not comply.

It did seem that Danny suffered from early neglect because his mother was an IV drug user and was heavily involved in this lifestyle for his first 3 years of life. Although his mother was able to hold down a job, throughout her drug use she was emotionally unavailable to Danny. Danny also suffered from frequent high fevers and ongoing ear infections from age 1 to approximately 3½ years old; thus, like so many other youngsters with chronic illnesses, he did not allow himself to be cuddled and nurtured.

Although the possibility of sexual abuse frequently had been brought up to Danny's mother since he had been in preschool, it was not substantiated until he began working on his past abuse history. Danny had been reported as having an extreme lack of boundaries, engaging in a great deal of "sexualized" talk, and having been involved on several occasions in sexualized behaviors with other children, including coercing other youngsters into the bathroom and removing clothing.

A good portion of Danny's therapy while in the Partial Hospital Program was geared toward assisting Danny to label and identify feelings, learning how to express his feelings in appropriate ways, and developing a greater sense of boundaries (emotional and physical). It was during this phase of his treatment that Danny disclosed the sexual abuse that had been occurring for years with two of his older cousins.

The following example was from a session that was held following a difficult morning with Danny in the Partial Hospital Program. He had gotten very verbally aggressive with his peers and staff and refused to discuss his feelings during group therapy. Assisting Danny to develop a "feelings journal" was an important part of his process because he had a very difficult time verbalizing his feelings. He seemed much more comfortable with drawing pictures and having someone act as his "secretary" in writing his words.

Example of Activity #65

Therapist Danny, it seems like you are having a difficult time today. It really seems like you are mad about something. Would you like to talk about what you are mad about?

Danny No, I don't have to talk to you about anything.

T You are right. You don't have to talk to me about anything. But you know that letting go of your angry feelings will help you to feel better and make better choices. So do you want to draw a picture to help you let go of your feelings?

D Yeah, I'll draw a picture but I'm not going to talk about it.

T That's okay. (Danny then proceeded to draw the picture.)

D There. I'm done.

T Wow, looks like you are pretty angry right now. Who is this a picture of?

D This is a picture of me. I'm killing myself because I am very angry.

T What are you so angry about that you feel like killing yourself?

D Would you write the words on my picture for me?

T Sure, what do you want me to write?

D This is a picture of me killing myself because I was very, very mad this morning. I was mad that I didn't get to go swimming. And I don't get to go to McDonald's.

T Well, what happened this morning that left you feeling so angry?

D I don't know. I've just been feeling that way. I got in trouble with my mom this morning and then I got in trouble when I got here.

The remainder of the session was spent discussing Danny's angry feelings. What eventually came out during the session was that one of Danny's cousins had come over to his house the night before, and Danny disclosed that he recently had told his mother about their (he and the cousin's) past sexual interactions. Apparently the cousin had previously threatened to "disown" Danny if he ever told anyone.

Danny was able to say that he was feeling very sad and scared that his cousin was actually going to follow through on his past threat. This session ended with Danny agreeing to discuss this with his mother in the family session that was being held in the evening.

Clinical Impressions: It is clear from Danny's drawing that he is an angry, confused child (see Illustration 9.2). However, it would be a mistake to jump to the conclusion that this was a suicidal message. It is important to clarify what pictures mean to the child who has drawn them. In this particular case, Danny indicated that this was an expression of his anger at his mom for not going swimming and not being able to go to McDonald's.

Clinically, he was displacing his anger at others onto himself. When this was discussed, he was able to express his feelings about a much deeper subject. At this time, Danny disclosed prior sexual abuse by his older cousin.

Danny had been threatened that he would be "disowned" if he ever told. This threat most likely cued abandonment issues from a father who had died from a drug overdose when he was a baby. In addition, his mother's emotional absence in his early years due to her drug addiction could have also been perceived as abandonment by him.

Pool

Illustration 9.2.

Danny and his mother had done a lot of work on feelings and building a more trusting relationship. He had been in therapy for at least 6 months before he was able to disclose the prior sexual abuse.

This reveals how important it is to work on the first stages of recovery (e.g., building trusting relationships) before some children allow themselves to express deeper wounds. He had been making very good progress on presenting issues (loss of father figure and abandonment issues) but seemed "stuck" at this point in his day-to-day functioning. It wasn't clear until he revealed this "secret" what was holding him back.

This case is a good example of how trauma resolution work can have its ebb and flow. Danny and his mother were doing well and now they were back to working on exploring the new revelation of sexual abuse. Treatment at this point shifted to exploring the sexual abuse trauma and included that in the overall treatment of this severely damaged child.

It is important to note that when something like this happens, you don't necessarily need to move back to square one and start over again at Phase I. For many children, you just need to go back a step or so to where they are at with the new information, incorporating it into their overall treatment.

❏ **Activity #66: Trina's Story**

Objective: To explore some of the healthy and unhealthy ways to express anger through the medium of storytelling.

This activity is designed to introduce and explore some of the healthy and unhealthy ways children express anger. It is common for abused children to harbor unresolved feelings that manifest themselves through anger and rage. These children typically need to develop and practice healthy skills of expressing feelings.

The story of Trina explores how one child was able to move from unhealthy expressions of anger to healthier means of expressing herself without hurting others. Many of the examples used in this story are common to abused children. Therefore, while reading the story, it will be important to process with the child regarding his or her "typical" coping skills.

Ages: This activity is designed for children ages 6 to 12.

Materials Needed: Activity sheet and pencils, crayons, colored pencils, and/or markers.

Instructions: Instruct the child to read or listen to the story of Trina. After reading the story, instruct the child to complete the questions related to the story. Process the questions with the child.

Note: The younger or nonreading child may need you to read the story to him or her.

Processing: After the child has finished reading the story, it is important to process the story and discuss the child's impressions. We have found it helpful to ask, "What do you think about the story?" "How did Trina feel in the story? Why?" "Have you ever felt like Trina? What did you do?"

❏ **Activity #67: My Contract**

Objective: To develop a plan to appropriately express and work through difficult feelings.

This activity is designed to assist the child in developing a plan to appropriately express and work through difficult feelings. The use of contracting is one way of empowering the child to develop a plan of action for future times when the child feels "stuck" with his or her feelings.

Contracting is not a new phenomenon. This therapeutic tool has been found to be extremely useful in assisting in creating change. When a child makes a promise to himself or herself and to the therapist, this can be a pivotal point in the healing process. The contract is individually designed to meet the unique needs of the child creating the contract.

In this particular contract activity, the child is asked to generate ways to take care of angry and hurt feelings.

Ages: Children ages 6 to 12 should have no problem coming up with ways to express themselves, such as writing, drawing, talking to someone, or doing a physical activity.

Materials Needed: Activity sheet and pencils.

Instructions: Instruct the child to think about the different ways of expressing feelings that have been explored in previous activities. Then have the child identify specific ways that he or she thinks will best help him or her to express angry or hurt feelings.

Once the child has identified the best ways to take care of difficult feelings, use the activity form to write these ideas into a contract.

Children who have difficulty writing may need to dictate their responses.

Processing: After the child has completed this activity, it is important to discuss the contract. We have found it helpful to ask, "Tell me about your contract." "What do you think might get in the way of doing some of these things? Why?" "What things do you think will be the most helpful? Why?"

❑ **Activity #68: Beginning My Journal**

Objective: To learn how to journal thoughts and feelings.

This activity is designed to help children develop a tool that can assist them on a lifelong journey as a survivor. Journaling thoughts and feelings can be extremely insightful and therapeutic. Writing down feelings really can help with obsessional thoughts that continue to haunt the child. This serves to move the thoughts and feelings from the head to the paper, which makes it more tangible and easier for the child to handle.

It is important for you as the therapist to realize that this is just the beginning of learning the journaling process. In order for the child to use this tool, he or she will need to be encouraged to "practice" this exercise outside of the therapy sessions. Once a child really learns this tool, it can be invaluable.

Ages: This activity is designed for children ages 6 to 12 who are able to express themselves in writing.

Materials Needed: Activity sheet, pencils, additional paper if needed, crayons, and so on if the child is drawing feelings.

Instructions: Instruct the child to write down or dictate his or her feelings for that day. Encourage the child to express why he or she is having the particular feelings. Also, you might want to encourage the child to write any additional thoughts he or she is having.

Note: A child who has difficulty writing may choose to draw pictures.

Processing: After the child has completed this activity, it is important to discuss the journal entry. We have found it helpful to ask, "Tell me about your journal entry." "How did you feel while writing about your feelings today?" "How do you think writing about your feelings can help you? Why?" "Is there anything else you want to add to your journal?"

The following case example will illustrate how one emotionally, physically, and sexually abused child processed this activity.

Case Example: *Jake*

Brief Case History: Jake was an 8-year-old who lived with his foster-adoptive mother when he was referred to the 3-hour Partial Hospital Program due to his out-of-control, overactive, aggressive, oppositional, defiant, and sexualized behaviors. Jake previously had been in therapy with an outpatient therapist for approximately a year; however, his acting-out behaviors escalated when two other children were placed in his home.

The most concerning escalation of his problematic behaviors was his sexual acting out. Prior to the two younger children being placed in the home, Jake had not been engaging in what his foster mother considered "sexual acting out." After the younger children came into the home, Jake exposed himself to them, trying to coerce them into showing him their private parts and attempting to touch them as well. It also was reported that he masturbated on a regular basis.

Following his placement in the Partial Hospital Program and further exploration of his past behaviors in his foster mother's home, it seemed many of Jake's behaviors pointed to serious emotional difficulties and a possible history of sexual abuse. His past records did not indicate any sexual abuse history.

When Jake was first placed in his foster mother's home, he had been abusing the family's dog by placing items in its rectum; this was finally discovered when the dog began bleeding. In addition, Jake frequently smeared his feces on the walls in the bathroom and hallway, stripped off all of his clothing, lay in the middle of the floor in a fetal position, and masturbated. He would ask his foster mother if she was going to come in and sleep with him at night, "because that is what a mother is supposed to do."

Jake had been given up by his biological mother for adoption when he was 7 years old. She apparently made this decision when Child Protective Services became involved with the family. Reports had been made that she was negligent and had abandoned him.

Jake's biological mother was a dancer at a topless club and frequently would leave him with acquaintances for days at a time. She also would not show up to pick him up after school. Eventually, the school personnel became so frustrated with her ongoing abandonment and "no shows" that they called Child Protective Services. It was at this time that someone suggested that she give Jake up for private adoption. Shortly after CPS began investigating the family's situation, Jake's mother did turn to private adoption as her solution.

Jake went directly from being in his mother's "care" to his foster-adopt placement. The foster-adopt placement was given little information regarding Jake's previous abuse history and/or his acting-out behaviors. Shortly following his placement, Jake's foster mother realized that he needed additional support and got him into outpatient therapy.

When Jake initially began treatment in the 3-hour Partial Hospital Program, it was obvious that he was a highly intelligent and very cognitive young boy. This was extremely helpful when it came to assisting him in learning how to develop problem-solving skills and in doing any kind of cognitive restructuring.

Jake was highly guarded with his emotions and feelings. It seemed that any time an attempt was made to engage him in addressing his emotions, he would either dissociate and begin talking about things such as "how the Egyptian pyramids were made" or he would escalate his behaviors to the point of needing to be placed in time-out.

Initially, Jake was not attending the Partial Hospital Program every day. He was coming 3 days a week with a day off in between the days he attended. This made it extremely difficult for a youngster such as Jake to begin to address his emotions. Eventually, his treatment was increased to 5 days in a row. When this happened,

Jake was able to work through his resistance to deal with his feelings and began to make progress in decreasing his acting-out, aggressive, and sexualized behaviors.

The following example is taken from a session a few months into Jake's treatment. Jake was asked to begin keeping a journal of the abusive events that happened in his past as a way of gaining some sense of control presently. Initially, Jake was asked to keep his journal at the Partial Hospital Program so that each entry could be processed with his therapist. Eventually, Jake asked to take his journal home so that he could work on it with his adoptive mom.

Example of Activity #68

Prior to beginning this session, a discussion was held with Jake regarding the purpose of writing a journal and the hope that it would be a way to assist him in getting control of his impulses. Jake was willing to cooperate but also was able to verbalize his hesitation and fear.

Therapist Now we can start working on your journal, Jake. I want you to think back to a time when you were with your first mom. Then I want you to draw a picture and we can talk about it.

Jake Okay, but this is kinda hard for me. Sometimes I don't like thinking about my mom because it makes me sad. (Started to tear up.)

T I know it's hard Jake, but we have to find a way for you to let out your feelings so that you are not being hurtful to other people.

J I know. (Started to draw a picture. When he finished, the picture was discussed.)

T Can you tell me what was happening in this picture?

J This is me, and my mom spanking me. I was trying to get away. She was spanking me because I wasn't doing the right thing. Can you write the words for me? Sometimes I don't like to write.

T Sure, Jake. If you want me to write the words I can. That must have hurt when your mom would spank you. I bet it made you sad, too.

J   Uh huh. Sometimes she would hit me with a stick. When she hit
    it on a table it sounded like a gunshot.
T   Sounds like your mom would try to scare you by hitting the
    stick on the table.
J   Uh huh. Sometimes she would hit me with a belt. When she was
    really, really mad she would hit me with a stick with thorns.
T   Ouch! I bet that really hurt. How did it make you feel when your
    mom did all of this stuff?
J   I don't know. But it makes me sad to think of it right now.
T   I bet you kinda felt sad then, too. You probably had lots of other
    feelings then, too. You might even have lots of different feelings
    now.

Clinical Impressions: Throughout the activity, Jake attempted to stay
away from his feelings unless directed to state a feeling. Even then,
he would end up describing the event. He prefers to stay in his
current feeling state rather than process how he felt at the time of
the abuse. This points out his defense mechanism of intellectualizing his feelings.

The picture (see Illustration 9.3) is full of action, with his mother
hitting him. He chose to draw stick figures and seemed to portray
himself as a very small, helpless child, perhaps even a baby. This
may indicate his emotional fixation at the age of early childhood
when he was first abused.

Jake describes many different ways his mother had hurt him. He
states that he was hit with her hand, a belt, a stick, and a stick with
thorns. His description of the stick hitting the table and sounding
like a gunshot may indicate his hypervigilance at the time. He was
acutely aware of sounds and actions around him.

Jake blames himself for his mother's actions. This is a common
scenario with traumatized children. This may also be his way of
protecting himself from being abandoned. It is safer to think he
pushed her away than to think she gave him up willingly.

It seems Jake has many issues to work through. He needs to
continue processing his early childhood memories and the feelings
associated with these memories. He needs to allow himself to connect with these difficult feelings associated with the abuse if he is to
resolve this trauma successfully. Currently, he is stuck in compart-

Illustration 9.3.

mentalizing or "intellectualizing" his feelings, which may be one reason he continues to "act out" behaviorally.

Jake would benefit from learning more about what he does have control of in his life rather than focusing on his lack of control. He needs to see himself as being more empowered rather than focusing on his helplessness so that he can move forward.

❏ **Activity #69: You Hurt Me!**

Objective: To express feelings in the form of a letter.

This activity is designed to enable children to express their feelings toward the abuser in a direct but less threatening way. Writing a therapeutic letter allows the child to appropriately focus feelings on those who have hurt him or her and who have not kept the child safe.

As stated in the introduction to this chapter, when anger is turned inward, children may become depressed, self-destructive, and filled with self-blame, which may become self-hate. Equally dangerous is misdirected anger, which tends to get out of control. Confronting the abuser is a necessary aspect of healing; however, it does not need to be done with a direct encounter with the abuser. Writing a therapeutic letter has been found to be a powerful technique in this process.

Ages: This activity is designed for children ages 6 to 12. Children who have difficulty writing may need to dictate the letter. This activity may elicit a variety of feelings. As the therapist, you will want to be acutely aware of the child's feelings and reactions so that you can assist in processing feelings.

Materials Needed: Activity sheet and pencils.

Instructions: Instruct the child to think about the things he or she would like to be able to say to the person(s) who hurt him or her. Then have the child either write or dictate a letter to the person(s) who caused the hurt. Encourage the child to include specifically what the person(s) did, how the child felt then and now, and what he or she would like to be able to do with the feelings.

Note: It is not uncommon for children to become very graphic in their descriptions of what they would like to do to the person(s). It is important to allow the child to express and fully process his or her thoughts and feelings.

Processing: After the child has completed his or her letter, it is important to process the letter by asking, "Tell me about your letter." "How did it feel to write the letter? Why?" "How does it feel to express your feelings to the person(s) who hurt you? Why?" "Is there anything else you would like to add to your letter?"

PHASE IV

Becoming Future Oriented

10

What Have I Learned?

When the child reaches this point, he or she has attained many goals in the healing process. The child's feelings should be at a fairly stable level. Therefore, the overwhelming feelings of victimization have subsided, allowing the child to focus on present living versus past experiences. When the child is at this point, the task becomes learning the skills to move forward successfully.

It is important to point out that the healing process cannot be rushed. There are no clear definitions of beginning and ending points. Some children will need to repeat all of the prior stages or some of the stages before they will have resolved their early traumas.

The purpose of this chapter is to have children assess what they have learned about their abuse and to identify the new skills they have acquired in completing these activities. Once the child has integrated this new learning into his or her day-to-day living, the child will feel more balanced. There will be movement from feelings of fragmentation to a sense of feeling whole.

The activities in this chapter are designed to assist the child in reviewing the many goals they have obtained in completing their healing process. In assisting the child with the activities in this chapter, you may gain some insight as to whether it is necessary to repeat any of the activities from the previous chapters. If it seems as though the child still struggles with particular issues, you may decide to repeat some of the previous activities particular to his or her needs.

❏ **Activity #70: Pride List**

Objective: To identify therapeutic accomplishments.

This activity is designed to encourage children to identify their therapeutic accomplishments. Abusive experiences can be so damaging to self-esteem that it can be difficult for individuals to acknowledge their progress toward a healthier, more integrated sense of self.

Ages: Although this activity is designed for children ages 6 through 12, you may find that processing with the child prior to beginning the activity will be helpful. Because abused children often are stuck in their abusive experiences, a discussion of progress will assist the child to focus on positive changes and personal growth. The child who has difficulty writing may choose to draw pictures or dictate his or her responses.

Materials Needed: Activity sheet and pencils, crayons, markers, and/or colored pencils.

Instructions: Instruct the child to think about all the hard work he or she has done so far. Ask him or her to think about all the new things that have been learned and what makes him or her feel proud. Then have the child list or draw pictures of things that make him or her feel proud.

Processing: After the child has completed the pride list, it is important to discuss the list by asking, "Tell me about the things that make you feel proud." "Which one of the things you listed are you most proud of? Why?" "Of the new things you have learned, which one do you think is the most important? Why?"

❑ Activity #71: I Am Special!

Objective: To be able to list positive self-attributes.

This activity is designed to assist children in integrating those things listed in Activity #70 with skills or attributes that now can be found within themselves. It is important to assist the child in this integration process so that these skills or attributes become part of the child's "core." It is hoped that this will assist in the process of strengthening the child's sense of self.

Ages: Children ages 6 to 12 should be able to complete this activity.

Materials Needed: Activity sheet and pencils, crayons, markers, and/or colored pencils.

Instructions: Instruct the child to think about all the new things that have been learned and make him or her proud. Then ask the child to think about what things he or she likes about himself or herself and that make the child feel special. Next, have the child write or draw the things that he or she likes about himself or herself.

Note: The younger child or the child with processing difficulties may need assistance linking or connecting these two activities. Therefore, a discussion helping to integrate these activities may be helpful prior to beginning this activity.

Processing: After the child has completed this activity, it is important to discuss the list by asking, "Tell me about the things you have learned that make you feel proud." "What things make you feel special?" "Of the things you listed or drew, which one do you like the most? Why?" "Is there anything else you want to add to your list? What?"

❏ Activity #72: Things I've Learned

Objective: To be able to list things that have been learned.

This activity is designed to assist the child in exploring and organizing the things that have been learned after completing the activities.

Ages: Children of all ages are capable of identifying the things they have learned.

Instructions: Instruct the child to think about what he or she feels are the most important things that have been learned after finishing the activities. Then have the child write or draw the most important things that have been learned.

Materials Needed: Activity sheet and pencils, crayons, markers, and/or colored pencils.

Note: The older or more emotionally mature child will be able to identify in more depth the things that were learned, but the younger child will need assistance. The younger child may choose to draw or dictate his or her responses.

Processing: After the child has completed this activity, it is important to discuss things that have been learned. We have found it helpful to ask, "Tell me about the things you have learned." "Which one of these things do you think is the most important? Why?" "Which one of these things do you think will be the most helpful to you? Why?" "Would you like to add anything else to your list?"

The following case example will illustrate how one drug-exposed, neglected, and physically abused child processed this activity.

Case Example: *Tyrone*

Brief Case History: Tyrone was a 6-year-old who was referred to the Early Childhood Partial Hospital Program for the second time over a 2-year period. Tyrone was living with his 23-year-old aunt, who had taken custody of him at age 2½.

Tyrone's biological mother was multiply addicted, used many substances, and prostituted throughout her pregnancy with him. Tyrone was born addicted and spent his first 3 months in withdrawal treatment. Tyrone lived with his mother until he was 2½ years old.

Eventually, Tyrone's mother was incarcerated for parole violation after she fled to another state. She left the state after she was reported to Child Protective Services. She was reported for child abuse again in the other state. Tyrone was placed with his aunt after his mother was arrested for crossing state lines without permission.

While in his mother's custody, Tyrone appeared traumatized not only by her lack of nurturing but also by physical and emotional abuse. It was reported that Tyrone was left unattended for hours while his mother continued to use substances and prostitute. This occurred from the time he was born until he was removed from his mother's care.

His mother apparently would lock him in dark closets and/or rooms while she would go out. She would strike him for spilling his food or not following her directives. Tyrone's mother also would frequently call him names, cuss, and belittle him.

By the time Tyrone was placed in his aunt's care, he was fearful to attempt anything. This included playing, eating, talking, sleeping, and so on. Tyrone was an overly anxious boy who would frequently throw temper tantrums and have screaming episodes lasting up to 2 hours at a time.

Tyrone's initial placement in the Partial Hospital Program was over a year in length. At that time, he was considered "asocial" or "schizoid-like," not desiring to have any contact with others, which included looking, touching, talking, or playing. He was very aggressive with other children and program staff.

On occasion, Tyrone would become very aggressive with other children and would physically attack them. He often needed to be restrained when he pinched, scratched, hit, and kicked peers/staff. Restraints were also frequently used when Tyrone was redirected in any way, because he would often become very angry, upset, and out of control.

By the time he was discharged, Tyrone had made enough progress to attend a special needs preschool classroom at a public school. However, following the end of the school year, his aunt did not enroll him in any summer programs. Thus, when the next school year began, Tyrone again showed signs of being extremely fearful and overly anxious.

He also was having severe sleep disturbances, reporting fears associated with nightmares and monsters and becoming increasingly oppositional. Tyrone again was admitted to the Partial Hospital Program for a brief period and transitioned to public school.

The following example was taken from a session held at the end of Tyrone's second Partial Hospital Placement. He again had stabilized, his fears were significantly reduced, and he was functioning well enough to be discharged with outpatient aftercare.

Example of Activity #72

Tyrone was asked to come to the therapist's office. Once inside the office, the first 10 minutes were spent playing with toys of his choice. Once the timer went off, he began the activity.

Therapist Tyrone, you know it is almost time for you to leave the program and go back to your other school.

Tyrone I know.

Th How are you feeling about that?

T Happy and scared.

Th It's normal to have different feelings when you are starting something new. But you've started a new school before, remember?

T Yeah, it was okay.

Th I know you'll do great at your new school because you know how to take care of your feelings.

T Most of the time.

Th Today I would like for you to think of all the things you can do now to take care of your mad, sad, and scared feelings. We can make it into a book if you want.

T Okay, I want red for the outside.

Th What is the first thing you know you can do to take care of your feelings?

T I can take a time-out when I am mad.

Th Yes, you can take a time-out when you are mad. I'm just going to write that on this page. You can draw your pictures when we are done, okay?

T Okay.

Th What else can you do to take care of your feelings?

T I can hit my pillow when I am mad.

Th Okay, anything else?

T I can go to a sit-out.

Th Okay, anything else?

T I can use my words.

Th Yes, you can use your words now! Is there anything else?

T I can laugh.

Th You can laugh? (Tyrone nodded) I am so glad to hear you say that it is okay for you to laugh. I think that is my favorite one!

T I can ask for help.

Th You mean from an adult? (Tyrone nodded) Okay, and what else?

T I can talk to my teachers. I'm done.

Th Okay, Tyrone, you really did a lot of hard work today. Is there anything special you would like to play with in my office?

Clinical Impressions: Given this child's significant abuse history, especially at such a young age, it is obvious he has made a great deal of progress in his recovery process. It seems Tyrone has learned how to trust others enough that he is able to verbalize reassurance that he will get help when he needs it.

In addition, it appears that Tyrone has developed a healthier sense of self. He is able to clearly state the things he can do to take care of himself. He has developed some sense of his own control, which may be what has helped him to reduce his fears and acting-out behaviors.

Tyrone no longer appears asocial or schizoid-like, in that he has become much more social. Clearly, he was so traumatized by his early abuse that he avoided social interactions due to previous painful consequences inflicted by his mother.

It is important to note that Tyrone most likely will go through many regressions in his lifetime. This is a "normal" process for children who have experienced severe trauma at such an early age. As children mature and develop, they will most likely show some signs of emotional regression. This should be viewed as a product of the maturation process versus a failure of previous therapy.

Tyrone is ready to face life's next challenges. He most likely will need to receive intermittent therapeutic support throughout his adolescence. He also will need to continue to be in a healthy, calm, and emotionally stable environment so that he can continue growing in a healthy way. This case points out just how damaged a child can be from such early trauma, as well as the need for intermittent therapeutic intervention over a life span.

❏ **Activity #73: Me Today!**

Objective: To draw a picture of self as seen after completing activities in this book.

This activity is designed to help you assess how children now see themselves. This activity also can be beneficial in revealing to children their own growth. You can facilitate this process by having the child compare this activity to the self-portrait portrayed in Activity #2 in Chapter 2.

Ages: Children ages 6 through 12 should be able to complete this activity with very little help.

Materials Needed: Activity sheet and pencils, crayons, markers, and/or colored pencils.

Instructions: Instruct the child to draw a picture of how he or she sees himself or herself today. Encourage the child to be as complete as possible.

Note: The older, more mature child will be more detailed in his or her drawing. However, there most likely will be a change in the two self-portraits, regardless of the age or functioning level of the child.

Processing: After the child has completed the drawing, it is important to discuss the drawing by asking, "Tell me about your drawing." "Tell me how you feel in this picture. Why?" "How is this picture different from the picture you drew in Activity #2? Why?"

❏ Activity #74: My Journal

Objective: To make a journal to use on a daily basis to express thoughts and feelings.
    This activity is designed to help children create a journal that they can use on a daily basis to express thoughts and feelings. The child may write words, draw pictures, cut and paste, or use any other means to express thoughts or feelings.
    This activity is for children to develop a lifelong skill of taking care of their thoughts and feelings. Children can make their own journal or use a spiral notebook.

Materials Needed: Purchase a spiral notebook or provide materials to create the child's own journal, such as construction paper, manila folders, writing paper, and so on.

Instructions: Instruct the child to begin a journal to keep his or her daily thoughts and feelings.

References

Achenback, T. M. (1991). *Manual for the Child Behavior Checklist/4-18 and 1991 Profile.* Burlington: University of Vermont, Department of Psychiatry.

American Professional Society on the Abuse of Children (APSAC). (1995). Psychosocial evaluation of suspected psychological maltreatment in children and adolescents. *Practice guidelines* (pp. 1-12). Chicago, IL: APSAC.

American Psychiatric Association. (1994). *Diagnostic and statistical manual of mental disorders* (4th ed.). Washington, DC: Author.

Bass, E., & Davis, L. (1988). *The courage to heal: A guide for women survivors of child sexual abuse.* New York: Perennial Library.

Berliner, L., & Conte, J. (1995). The effects of disclosure and intervention on sexually abused children. *Child Abuse & Neglect, 19*(3), 371-384.

Bolton, F., & Bolton, S. (1987). *Working with violent families.* Newbury Park, CA: Sage.

Briere, J. (1989). *Therapy for adults molested as children: Beyond survival.* New York: Springer.

Briere, J. (1992). *Child abuse trauma: Theory and treatment of the lasting effects.* Newbury Park, CA: Sage.

Briere, J., & Conte, J. (1993). Self-reported amnesia for abuse in adults molested as children. *Journal of Traumatic Stress, 6*(1), 21-31.

Briere, J., & Runtz, M. (1989). The Trauma Symptom Checklist (TSC-33): Early data on a new scale. *Journal of Interpersonal Violence, 4,* 151-163.

Burgess, A. W., & Holmstrom, L. (1978). Accessory-to-sex: Pressure, sex, and secrecy. In A. W. Burgess, A. N. Groth, L. L. Holmstrom, & S. M. Sgroi (Eds.), *Sexual assault of children and adolescents* (pp. 85-98). Lexington, MA: Lexington Books.

223

Conte, J., Briere, J., & Sexton, D. (1989, August). *Moderators of the long-term effects of sexual abuse.* Paper presented at the annual meeting of the American Psychological Association, New Orleans, LA.

Courtois, C. A. (1988). *Healing the incest wound: Adult survivors in therapy.* New York: Norton.

Crowley, R. J., & Mills, J. C. (1989). *Cartoon magic.* New York: Brunner/Mazel.

Cunningham, C., & MacFarlane, K. (1991). *When children molest children: Group treatment strategies for young sexual abusers.* Orwell, VT: Safer Society Press.

Doris, J. (Ed.). (1991). *The suggestibility of children's recollections.* Washington, DC: American Psychological Association.

Elliott, D. M., & Briere, J. (1992). Sexual abuse trauma among professional women: Validating the Trauma Symptom Checklist-40 (TSC-40). *Child Abuse & Neglect, 16,* 391-398.

Elson, M. (1987). *The Kohut seminars on self-psychology and psychotherapy with adolescents and young adults.* New York: Norton.

Everstine, D. S., & Everstine, L. (1989). *Sexual trauma in children and adolescents.* New York: Brunner/Mazel.

Finkelhor, D., & Associates. (Ed.). (1986). *A sourcebook on child sexual abuse.* Beverly Hills, CA: Sage.

Finkelhor, D., & Browne, A. (1986). Initial and long-term effects: A conceptual framework. In D. Finkelhor & Associates (Eds.), *A sourcebook on child sexual abuse* (pp. 180-198). Beverly Hills, CA: Sage.

Finkelhor, D., Hotaling, G., Lewis, I. A., & Smith, C. (1989). Sexual abuse and its relationship to later sexual satisfaction, marital status, religion, and attitudes. *Journal of Interpersonal Violence, 4,* 279-399.

Friedrich, W. N. (1990). Developmental considerations. In W. N. Friedrich (Ed.), *Psychotherapy of sexually abused children and their families.* New York: Norton.

Friedrich, W. N. (1995). *Psychotherapy with sexually abused boys.* Thousand Oaks, CA: Sage.

Fromuth, M. E. (1986). The relationship of childhood sexual abuse with later psychological and sexual adjustment in a sample of college women. *Child Abuse & Neglect, 10,* 5-16.

Garbarino, J., Guttman, E., & Seeley, J. (1986). *The psychologically battered child: Strategies for identification, assessment and intervention.* San Francisco: Jossey-Bass.

Gil, E. (1991). *The healing power of play: Therapy with abused children.* New York: Guilford.

Gil, E. (1992, October). *Treatment of abused and sexualized children.* Workshop presented in Boise, ID.

Gil, E., & Johnson, T. C. (1993). *Sexualized children: Assessment and treatment of sexualized children and children who molest.* Rockville, MD: Launch Press.

Haugaard, J. J., & Reppucci, N. D. (1988). *The sexual abuse of children.* San Francisco: Jossey-Bass.

Helfer, R. E. (1987). The developmental basis of child abuse and neglect: An epidemiological approach. In R. E. Helfer & R. S. Kempe (Eds.), *The battered child* (4th ed., pp. 60-80). Chicago: University of Chicago Press.

Helfer, R. E., & Kempe, R. S. (1987). *The battered child* (4th ed.). Chicago: University of Chicago Press.

Henschel, D., Briere, J., Magallanes, M., & Smiljanich, K. (1990, April). *Sexual abuse related attributions: Probing the role of "traumagenic factors."* Paper presented at the annual meeting of the Western Psychological Association, Los Angeles.

Herman, J. (1981). *Father-daughter incest.* Cambridge, MA: Harvard University Press.

Jessie. (1991). *Please tell! A child's story about sexual abuse.* Center City, MN: Hazelden Foundation.

Karp, C. (1995). The repressed memory controversy. *Family Advocate, 17*(3), 70-71. Chicago: ABA Family Law Section.

Karp, L., & Karp, C. (1989). *Domestic torts: Family violence, conflict and sexual abuse.* Colorado Springs, CO: Shepard's/McGraw-Hill.

Kaufman, B., & Wohl, A. (1992). *Casualties of childhood: A developmental perspective on sexual abuse using projective drawings.* New York: Brunner/Mazel.

Kohut, H. (1971). *The analysis of the self.* New York: International Universities Press.

Kohut, H. (1977). *The restoration of the self.* Madison, CT: International Universities Press.

MacFarlane, K., Waterman, J., with Conerly, S., Damon, L., Durfee, M., & Long, S. (1986). *Sexual abuse of young children.* New York: Guilford.

Malchiodi, C. (1990). *Breaking the silence: Art therapy with children from violent homes.* New York: Brunner/Mazel.

Martinson, F. M. (1991). Normal sexual development in infancy and childhood. In G. D. Ryan & S. L. Lane (Eds.), *Juvenile sexual offending.* Lexington, MA: Lexington Books.

Mayer, M. (1986). *There's a nightmare in my closet.* New York: A Pied Piper Book.

Mayer, M. (1988). *There's something in my attic.* New York: A Pied Piper Book.

Mills, J. C., & Crowley, R. J. (1986). *Therapeutic metaphors for children and the child within.* New York: Brunner/Mazel.

National Adolescent Perpetrator Network. (1988). Preliminary report from the National Task Force on Juvenile Sexual Offending 1988. *Juvenile & Family Court Journal, 39*(2), 1-67.

Peters, S. D. (1988). Child sexual abuse and later psychological problems. In G. E. Wyatt & G. J. Powell (Eds.), *Lasting effects of child sexual abuse* (pp. 108-118). Newbury Park, CA: Sage.

Santostefano, S., & Calicchia, J. A. (1992). Body image, relational psychoanalysis, and the construction of meaning: Implications for treating aggressive children. *Development and Psychopathology, 4,* 655-678.

Sgroi, S. M. (1982). *Handbook of clinical intervention in child sexual abuse.* Lexington, MA: Lexington Books.

Sgroi, S. M. (1988). *Vulnerable populations* (Vol. 1). Lexington, MA: Lexington Books.

Stern, D. (1985). *The interpersonal world of the infant: A view from psychoanalysis and developmental psychology.* New York: Basic Books.

Terr, L. (1990). *Too scared to cry: Psychic trauma in childhood.* New York: Harper & Row.

Terr, L. (1994). *Unchained memories: True stories of traumatic memories, lost and found.* New York: Basic Books.

Webb, N. B. (1991). *Play therapy with children in crisis.* New York: Guilford.

Wiese, D., & Daro, D. (1995). *Current trends in child abuse reporting and fatalities: The results of the 1994 Annual Fifty States Survey.* Chicago: National Committee to Prevent Child Abuse.

Zivney, O. A., Nash, M. R., & Hulsey, T. L. (1988). Sexual abuse in early versus late childhood: Differing patterns of pathology as revealed on the Rorschach. *Psychotherapy, 25,* 99-106.

Index

About the Authors

Cheryl L. Karp, PhD, is Clinical Director of the Trauma Program at Desert Hills Center for Youth and Families, a youth psychiatric hospital and residential treatment center, in Tucson, Arizona. She is a graduate of the University of Arizona (1978) and has been in

 private practice as a licensed psychologist since 1980, specializing in sexual and physical abuse issues and forensic psychology, with a clinical emphasis on the effects of trauma.

Dr. Karp has coauthored a book with her attorney husband, Leonard Karp, *Domestic Torts: Family Violence, Conflict and Sexual Abuse* (1989, Supp. 1996). She serves on the editorial board of *Divorce Litigation* and speaks and writes on the subjects of domestic torts, Battered Woman Syndrome, child abuse, posttraumatic stress, and the psychologist as expert in forensic cases. She has consulted to Child

Protective Services (CPS), the Department of Public Safety, and the Department of Corrections. She is an active member of the American Professional Society on the Abuse of Children (APSAC) and has served as president of the Arizona chapter. She is also a member of the American Psychological Association.

Traci L. Butler received her master's degree from the University of Arizona in Counseling and Guidance in 1989. She is a National Certified Counselor and is currently in private practice and is a school counselor for Tucson Unified School District. Prior to this, she was employed as a family thera-  pist and Assistant Director of the Early Childhood Program at Desert Hills Center for Youth and Families in Tucson, Arizona. This program specialized in providing early prevention and intervention for children ages 2 through 11.

Butler was formerly a special educator for 5 years working with children who were experiencing severe emotional difficulties. She also consults with a residential treatment facility for women substance abusers and their children and facilitates groups for teenage mothers to assist in developing parenting skills. She has presented at workshops and conferences on the issues of child abuse and parenting.